W9-CFL-953

A TRUE LEGACY

BY DAVE ANDERSON

JOE PATERNO'S LEGACY isn't his won-lost record at Penn State. His legacy is himself.

His impact on his players. His integrity. His instinct. His guts to do the right thing.

That legacy developed as early as The Coach's fourth season when he suddenly was surrounded by the flames of a national controversy with the President of the United States.

But he never flinched.

As his undefeated 1969 team (with Franco Harris, Lydell Mitchell and Jack Ham) awaited its Orange Bowl game with Missouri for the mythical national title, President Richard M. Nixon awarded a No. 1 trophy to Texas after its late-season 15-14 victory over Arkansas. Another coach might have tried to laugh off the President's premature presentation, especially when Nixon offered to provide Penn State with a political panacea, a plaque honoring its 21-game winning streak and 29-game unbeaten streak.

Joseph Vincent Paterno, out of Brooklyn and Brown

University, was not amused or impressed.

"Before accepting such a plaque," he said, "I would have to confer with my squad. I'm sure they would be disappointed at this time, as would the Missouri squad, to receive anything other than a plaque for the No. 1 team. And the No. 1 team following the bowl games, could be Penn State or Missouri. It would seem a waste of [the President's] valuable time to present Penn State with a plaque for something we already have undisputed possession of — the nation's longest winning and unbeaten streaks."

The Nittany Lions won that Orange Bowl game, 10-3, for their second straight 11-0 record, but finished second in that season's final Associated Press and United Press International polls.

"I don't like to be pushing this thing," The Coach said then, "but I still think we have as much right to be No. 1 as Texas or anybody else. Why should I sit back and let the President of the United States say that so-and-so is No. 1 when I've got 50 kids who've worked their tails off for me for three years. People can say it's sour grapes, but I'd be a lousy coach if I didn't argue for my team. When President Nixon stuck his two cents in, he took something away from my kids before the bowls."

Usually, the President's opinion is sometimes worth millions, if not billions, of dollars in economic matters, but to Joe Paterno, it was only worth two cents.

Years later, after Nixon resigned as President during the Federal investigation over the burglarizing of the Democratic national headquarters at the Watergate apartment complex in the nation's capital, The Coach had the last word.

"It mystifies me," he said, "how much Nixon knew about college football in 1969 and how little he knew about Watergate in 1973."

Joe Paterno is as blunt as his rolled-up pants legs and white socks on the sideline, as basic as the Penn State uniforms. He didn't design them, but he's never considered changing them. White helmets with a blue stripe down the middle. Blue jerseys with white numbers on the back and high on the sleeves, or white jerseys with blue numbers. White pants. White socks. Black shoes. But in today's flashy football fashions, it's not what the uniforms are so much as what they are not. No logos on the helmet. No names on the jerseys. No stripes on the sleeves or the pants.

"I think our uniforms say something to kids," The Coach has said, "about team-oriented play and an austere approach to life."

Those blue-and-white uniforms also keep saying something to kids and everybody else about how Joe Paterno is different.

Too many other college coaches wink at the NCAA recruiting and eligibility rules or jump to the NFL at the drop of a multimillion-dollar offer.

But he has always measured the importance of his role on the University Park campus against the temptation of mere money beyond the campus.

"More than anything else, coaches are teachers," he has said. "We have the same obligation as all teachers at our institutions, except we probably have more influence over our young people than anyone other than their families. We're dealing with discipline and loyalty and pride. The things that make a difference in a person's life — pride, loyalty and commitment — are the things that make a difference in this country. We're teaching them the realities of the competitive life."

Teaching those realities by example. Win or lose, The Coach has lived those realities.

"His philosophy was that college was getting an education first," John Skorupan, an All-America linebacker in 1972, said. "I think we always felt we had someone special in Joe Paterno. I was part of the Grand Experiment — that football players can get an education, that they can talk, that they're not dumb jocks."

But it didn't take long for the NFL to covet The Coach of that Grand Experiment.

When the New England Patriots pursued him after that 1972 team lost the Sugar Bowl game, he actually agreed to an offer involving salary, bonuses and franchise stock. But at the Plaza Hotel in New York the night before a morning meeting there to go over the language of the contract with his attorney and the club's attorneys, he couldn't sleep. At five-thirty that morning, he phoned Billy Sullivan, the Patriots' owner.

"I'm sorry to wake you up," The Coach told him, "but I wanted to get you before you left for New York and tell you that I've changed my mind."

He realized, as he later acknowledged, "that I was going to take it just for the money." And to him, unlike most people, the money wasn't that important. Certainly not as important as remaining at Penn State

where he and his wife Sue were raising their five children: Diana, Mary Kathryn, David, Jay and Scott.

"My wife is comfortable here," he often said. "My kids are comfortable here. I'm comfortable here."

Inevitably, the NFL would tempt him again. As his 1978 team, then 11-0, awaited what would be a 14-7 loss to Alabama in the Sugar Bowl, the New York Giants contacted him. By then he knew how important it was for an NFL coach, such as Don Shula of the Miami Dolphins or Tom Landry of the Dallas Cowboys, to have what he had at Penn State — complete authority over the football program.

"It would take an unusual situation to get me to move out of here," he said at the time. "For me to go to the Giants or any NFL team, it would be a question of being able to be the boss when something has to be done."

In other words, it would be a question of his having an NFL general manager's authority in selecting players as well as coaching them. But even before Wellington Mara, the Giants president and co-owner, was willing to offer him the dual role, The Coach decided he was happy in Happy Valley.

"I told Mr. Mara," he explained after asking not to be considered by the Giants, "not to bother making me an offer I couldn't refuse."

In time, The Coach would develop two national championship teams, in 1982 and 1986, but he often minimized the importance of those mythical titles.

"If we win the national championship, so what?" he once said. "It sounds cornball, but that's the way I feel. Somebody once asked Knute Rockne which team was his best and he said, 'The future would determine that.' My best team will be the one that produces the best doctors, lawyers, fathers and citizens — not necessarily the one with the best record. Let's keep it in context."

Let's keep his legacy in context too.

As the 2000 season began, Joe Paterno had a 317-83-3 record, his 34 seasons at Penn State were the most for a coach at one college except for Amos Alonzo Stagg's 41 at the College of the Pacific, he was the only coach to have won all four major bowls (Rose, Sugar, Orange and Cotton), he had the winningest bowl record of any coach (20-9-1), he was the only four-time Coach of the Year as selected by the American Football Coaches Association, he had produced 55 first-team All-Americas, and he had developed more than 200 NFL players, including first-round draft choices.

Arguably more important, he had coached 20 first-team Academic All-Americas, 16 NCAA Postgraduate Scholarship Athletes and 13 National Football Hall of Fame Scholar-Athletes — not to mention all those players among the best doctors, lawyers, fathers and citizens that he had produced.

Nearly three decades ago, in ignoring Penn State's right to be No. 1 in the final polls, President Nixon discovered to his dismay that Joe Paterno was much more than a football coach.

But by the time The Coach's 1986 national champions were honored at the White House, he had established what he was all about. President Ronald Reagan, who once portrayed George Gipp in the movie about legendary Notre Dame coach Knute Rockne, understood that.

"Joe Paterno has never forgotten," President Reagan said, "that he is a teacher who is preparing his students not just for the season, but for life."

That's why Joe Paterno's legacy isn't just all those victories and all those bowl games and all those coach-of-the-year plaques and all those NFL players and all those honored student-athletes. That's why Joe Paterno's legacy is himself.

Brooklyn Prep linebacker Joe Paterno, wearing
No. 9, helps chase down an opposing player.
As a senior, he made his mark as a quarterback.

CHAPTER ONE

BY STEVE HALVONIK

ANGELO AND FLORENCE PATERNO'S first son was a stand-up Joe long before Penn State's "Grand Experiment" made him a nationally recognized spokesman for college football.

He was a student at Brown the night a couple of bullies were harassing two Jewish students and their dates at a Providence, R.I., diner.

Paterno jumped from his seat and yelled, "Hey, cut that out! Leave them alone."

A shoving match ensued, but Paterno held his ground and the bullies departed.

Paterno plays down the incident, but his friends say it tells a lot about the character of the man.

"Joe was a funny guy, but if he didn't think something was right or fair, he was very outspoken," says Martin Gresh, one of Paterno's old fraternity buddies and college teammates. "He's that kind of person. He always was for the underdog. He didn't like people being racist or any of that stuff."

Whether fighting for classmates at Brown or defending the honor of Eastern football, Paterno has always aligned himself squarely behind the underdog. Because that is how he has always viewed himself.

Paterno doesn't define himself by his coaching victories or national championships. Or by his awards and honors. Ask him who he is and he will invariably respond, "An Italian kid from Brooklyn."

Some may find the answer glib or shallow, but there is more than a grain of sincerity to it.

Like many members of his generation, Paterno is a product of the great wave of European immigration that swept over the United States in the late 19th and early 20th Centuries. He is old enough to have experienced the ethnic slurs and social slights that many Italians, Irish, Jews and Poles suffered in their struggles to assimilate and thrive in a new and sometimes hostile country.

Left, Angelo and Florence Paterno pose proudly with their firstborn son, Joseph Vincent. Above, Joe as a lad.

"My mother always said two things: Her parents came over here to be Americans, not Italians; and, we never want to forget we're Italians," Paterno says.

Paterno overcame but never forgot the emotional hurts he suffered: The taunts of "wop;" the young woman who jilted him on the dance floor after learning he was Italian; the snubs of upper-class WASP students at Brown.

"Joseph came from a neighborhood of ethnic rivalries and slurs," says Thomas Bermingham, a Catholic priest who became Paterno's mentor at Brooklyn Prep. "I could see the hurts he suf-

1930's: Joseph, right, and his brother George between games of stickball in the neighborhood.

at 15 months of age. The Paternos' fourth child, a daughter named Florence, was born when Joe was 9.

Angelo and Florence Paterno were typical of many second-generation American families trying to climb the ladder to success.

Although he was reared as an Italian, Angelo was actually of Albanian descent. Generations before his birth, his family moved to the Italian province of Calabria, at the toe of the Italian boot. Angelo was a Franklin Delano Roosevelt Democrat who played semi-pro football. He shared his love and knowledge of this quintessentially American sport with his two sons. When Joe started playing, he never asked, "Did you win?" but always, "Did you have fun?"

On Saturday afternoons, Angelo listened to live broadcasts of the Metropolitan Opera. When Joe became a football coach at Penn State, he drew up game plans while listening to opera.

In 1916, Angelo dropped out of high school and enlisted in the U.S. Army. He served under General Pershing, chasing Pancho Villa across Mexico. He then went to Europe to fight against the Germans in World War I.

After he was discharged, Angelo returned to New York. He worked during the day and finished high school at night. He decided to become a lawyer, and began taking night classes at St. John's University. This led to a clerical job in the Appellate Division of the New York State Supreme Court. He worked his way up to becoming a court clerk, a judge's chief administrative assistant. It didn't pay much, but at least Angelo Paterno had a job during the Great Depression.

The family of Florence de la Salle Paterno hailed from Naples, Italy. Her father moved to the United States before the turn of the century, when he was 16. From an immigrant's wages of less than $1 a day he scraped up enough money to return to Italy in his 30's and find the 15-year-old bride who was to become Joseph Vincent Paterno's grandmother.

Florence's parents returned to the United States and had 10 children. Her father bought a horse-drawn wagon and delivered cashews and peanuts on Long Island. The business grew, and Florence's father bought first one motorized truck and then another. The family settled in a tenement on Troy Avenue,

fered from people slurring his Italian background."

The values and principles that Paterno exhibited in turning Penn State into a model football program are deeply rooted in his Brooklyn childhood.

Joseph Vincent Paterno was born Dec. 21, 1926, on 18th Street in the Flatbush section of Brooklyn. Florence wanted to name him Angelo Lafayette Jr., in honor of his father.

"That led to a difference of opinion, one of the few arguments that my gentle dad ever won over my mother's powerful will," Paterno says in his 1989 autobiography, *Paterno: By the Book.*

So he became Joseph Vincent instead.

Twenty-one months after Joe was born, Angelo and Florence had a second child, George. A third son, Franklin, died

George

High School Bklyn Prep Joe

20

near Atlantic Avenue, in the Bedford-Stuyvesant section of Brooklyn.

Angelo and Florence Paterno shared a brownstone with members of Florence's family when Joseph was born in 1926. It was a mixed neighborhood, with white people living on one side of the street and black people on the other. As the neighborhood became more ethnically mixed, tensions rose, and the Paternos moved, but they remained in the same general neighborhood.

Angelo finally achieved his dream and became a lawyer in 1941, at the age of 44. Nevertheless, the Paternos remained a family of modest means. They always rented houses because Angelo could never afford to buy one.

They were renting a house on 23rd Street between Avenues S and T when Joe and George attended St. Edmond's Grammar School. It was a nice street, with lots of other children to play with. The Paterno boys played stickball in the street and their mother packed them lunches for all-day basketball games in the park. A baseball fan, Joe became an usher at Ebbets Field and watched the Dodgers from the outfield bleachers.

"I had a great childhood in Brooklyn," Paterno says.

When Joe was graduated from St. Edmond's, the family moved to 26th Street and Avenue R, just one block from James Madison High School. Madison was a good public high school, but Angelo Paterno wanted his sons to attend Brooklyn Prep, a private Catholic school run by Jesuits. Tuition was $200 a year for Joe. When it was time for George to attend Brooklyn Prep, Angelo went to see school administrators and negotiated a cut-rate price of $30 a month tuition for both sons.

"That was a lot of money for a man making $5,200 a year," Paterno says. "But that was my father: Everything for us."

To reach Brooklyn Prep, young Joe walked 10 blocks each morning to board a trolley that took him on a 40-minute ride to school. He was a skinny 125-pounder when he arrived on campus in February 1941.

[**Joe and his younger brother George were known as the "Gold Dust twins" at Brooklyn Prep, as the team lost only one game Joe's senior year.**]

George, left, and Joe pose for a picture during
Joe's senior season at Brooklyn Prep. Their
coach, Zev Graham, starred at Fordham.

He didn't see any varsity football action as a freshman, but as a sophomore he returned kicks for the special teams.

Brooklyn Prep got a new head football coach before Paterno's junior year — Zev Graham, a former All-America quarterback at Fordham. Graham started Paterno at guard on offense and at linebacker on defense, but the team won only two games.

It was quite a different story in Paterno's senior year. Brooklyn Prep emerged as the best Catholic-school team in New York, and Paterno blossomed into a standout player. He played fullback and quarterback and called the plays because

Graham was impressed with his football smarts.

The local papers dubbed Joe and George, who was a year behind, "the Gold Dust twins." Brooklyn Prep lost only one game Paterno's senior year — to St. Cecilia's High School of Englewood, N.J. St. Cecilia's was coached by Vince Lombardi, who would go on to greater glory as the Hall of Fame coach of the Green Bay Packers.

Even as a teen-ager, Paterno exhibited leadership qualities. Every year in school, he was a class officer, including class president, and was vice president of the student council. He also belonged to the Book Discussion Club and the Sodality Club, a religious discussion group that also did neighborhood charity work.

"Joe was always a class act," says Francis Mahoney, who attended Brooklyn Prep and Brown University with Paterno.

"He was a good high school athlete and an excellent scholar. He never had a big head."

Mahoney says Paterno clearly reflected the values and determination of his parents.

Paterno always has said that he got his drive and determination, as well as his outspokenness, from his mother. Besides the love of football and opera, his father taught him the value of education and the honor of self-sacrifice. Angelo also taught Joe to identify with the underdogs — the less fortunate members of society who struggle against long odds to achieve their dreams.

Joe was an 18-year-old Army private, serving in Korea, on Oct. 25, 1945, when Angelo delivered a sermon to an interfaith religious group on the need for brotherhood.

"One cannot proclaim affection for a person of another faith or color and then refuse that person admission to his society because he does not worship in the same church or because he happened to be born of colored parents," Angelo said. "All of the talking and all of the literature in behalf of tolerance are wasted energies unless accompanied by some overt acts of the proponents in furtherance of our principles."

Joe's sister, Florence, discovered a copy of Angelo's speech in some papers she found after her father's death. After reading the speech, Joe said he realized how much his father's moral philosophy had shaped his own.

Another major influence in Paterno's life was Father Bermingham, who, when they met, was an idealistic priest-in-training, or scholastic, at Brooklyn Prep. It was Bermingham who nurtured Paterno's intellectual curiosity and challenged him to reach his full potential.

"We're all products of the people we meet in our life," Paterno says. "Father Bermingham was a great influence."

Paterno met Bermingham during his junior year of high school, when he enrolled in Bermingham's Latin class. He was almost 17. It was the first class for Bermingham, 25, who was just embarking on a 13-year odyssey to becoming a Jesuit.

Father Bermingham was immediately impressed by young Joe's academic potential and invited Joe to study with him after school two or three afternoons a week. Paterno had to get permission from his varsity football and basketball coach-

Above, Thomas Bermingham, a Catholic priest who became Paterno's mentor at Brooklyn Prep. Below, Joe served in the U.S. Army during the final year of World War II.

Joe did it all at Brown, playing quarterback and and returning punts and kickoffs. He also played basketball for two seasons.

es to miss practice, but he attended the sessions with Father Bermingham faithfully.

"The way Joseph jumped at the chance to be further challenged was so unusual," Father Bermingham says. "He was so intellectually hungry."

Father Bermingham also taught George. He says he was amazed at how different the two Paterno boys were.

"George was a completely different character. He was almost an extrovert, and physically, he was antsy. He could hardly sit in the classroom. But Joseph was very calm, composed."

After meeting Angelo Paterno, who was president of the Fathers' Club at Brooklyn Prep, Father Bermingham said he realized that Joe took after his father.

"In many ways, they were the same. The father had such a balance in his life and philosophy. Joseph wouldn't have been the same person without the father he had."

Joe Paterno was a senior when Father Bermingham introduced him to the great Roman poet Virgil and his epic poem, the Aeneid. They read it together in Latin, all 400 pages, and young Joe was enthralled by its lessons of sacrifice and struggle in the pursuit of personal accomplishment.

"I don't think anybody can get a handle on what makes me tick as a person, and certainly can't get at the roots of how I coach football, without understanding what I learned from the deep relationship I formed with Virgil during those afternoons and later in my life," Paterno says.

Several years ago, Father Bermingham attended a football banquet at which Paterno was the keynote speaker. Paterno spoke about his coaching philosophy and how it was shaped by Virgil.

"The other coaches nodded, but I don't think they knew what Joe was talking about," Father Bermingham says with a hearty laugh.

Father Bermingham played another pivotal role in Joe's life, convincing Angelo Paterno that it was all right to let his elder son attend college at Brown.

Although Joe Paterno made the New York all-metropolitan football team his senior year, few colleges offered him athletic scholarships because of his unimpressive size. Angelo har-

bored dreams of Joe and George attending college together as a "package," but it seemed a long shot, at best. Fordham offered Joe a partial basketball scholarship and Boston College, another Catholic school, was interested in George, who still had a year to go at Brooklyn Prep, as a football player.

Just when Angelo's dream seemed hopeless, along came "Busy" Arnold.

Everett M. (Busy) Arnold was a comic-book publisher in New York. He also was a big booster of Brown University football, picking up the tuition tab for about a dozen players. In those days, it was permissible for fans and alumni to act as "sponsors" for athletes, paying their tuition and supplying them with spending money.

One day, Zev Graham pulled Paterno aside and said that Arnold was interested in paying for both Joe and George to attend Brown, an Ivy League school in Providence, R.I. Graham said he wanted to talk to Joe's father.

Arnold's offer posed a real quandary to Angelo Paterno. On the one hand, it fulfilled his dream of Joe and George attending college together, looking out for one another. On the other, Brown was not a Catholic institution. A devout Catholic, Angelo Paterno sought advice from several priests, who told him it was a sin for his sons to attend a secular college.

Finally, Angelo Paterno turned to Father Bermingham, who assured him that it would be OK for Joe to matriculate at Brown.

"I told him, 'Look, you don't have to worry about Joseph's deep-down faith,'" Father Bermingham says. "I told him that he should let Joseph go to Brown. I told him that Joseph deserved something more."

Angelo relented, but the decision became moot — at least for the time being — because Joe was drafted into the U.S. Army six weeks after graduation from Brooklyn Prep.

After basic training, Joe was shipped to Korea. He got an early discharge in the summer of 1946 so that he could play football at the U.S. Naval Academy. But once he was discharged, Paterno crossed up everyone and enrolled at Brown instead.

In the early years after World War II, Brown's blue-blood sensibilities were upset by ambitious young men attending col-

The "Gold Dust twins" glittered in college as well. With George, left, at fullback and Joe, right, at quarterback, Brown went 8-1 in 1949.

lege on the G.I. Bill. The Brown football team reflected the changing student population, with Jews, Italians, Irish and Slovaks dotting the roster.

Paterno joined Delta Kappa Epsilon fraternity, a popular house among Brown football players.

Joe and Martin Gresh, a Slovak and running back on the football team, waited tables together at the fraternity house. There was one fraternity brother who didn't like Paterno. He would quickly gobble down his meal and yell for Paterno to bring him seconds. Paterno didn't like the guy any more than he liked Joe. So one night, Paterno laced the man's mashed potatoes with sawdust.

"The guy ate them and never knew the difference," Gresh says. "But that was Joe. He was kind of a jokester and kidder,

except when it came to football. When he played football, he always showed his serious side. He worked hard at it. One year, he lost 30 pounds. He scared the coaches; they thought he was sick. But he studied hard and knew the game as well as any of the coaches."

Nevertheless, it took a while for Paterno to catch the coaches' attention. He spent his first season at Brown almost exclusively on defense, primarily at safety.

During the winter, Paterno suited up with the Brown men's varsity basketball team, lettering for the Bears his sophomore and junior seasons. His coach was Weeb Ewbank, who would later lead the New York Jets to a Super Bowl football championship in 1968.

When Paterno was a junior, Brown and rival Holy Cross entered their grudge match in Boston Garden with undefeated records. Holy Cross was led by a high-scoring guard named Bob Cousy. Paterno, who fancied himself a better basketball player than football player, approached Ewbank before the

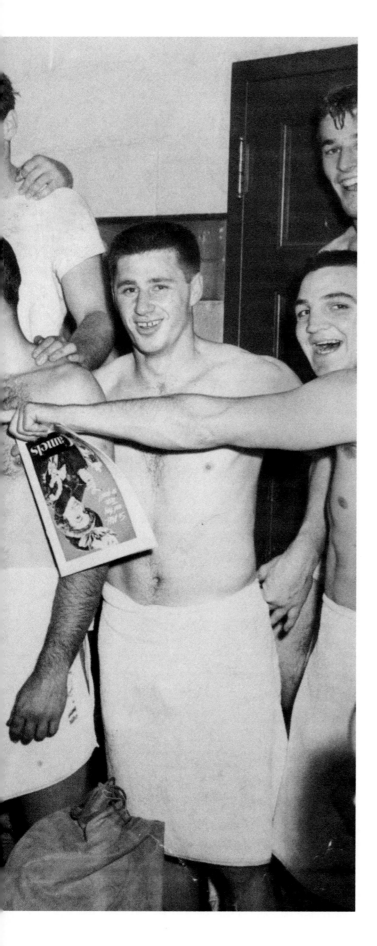

game and told him he could handle Cousy. Ewbank accepted Paterno's offer and started him. The taller, faster Cousy scorched Paterno for 10 points in the first minute-and-a-half. By halftime, Holy Cross led, 50-17, and Paterno was back on the bench.

On the football field, Paterno led the team in total yards for runbacks his junior season. His season's best was 146 yards returning punts and kicks in a 23-20 victory over Princeton.

Paterno was finally making an impression on his head coach, Rip Engle, a quiet, reserved 40-year-old who looked older than his years because of his prematurely gray hair and his penchant for wearing fedoras on the sideline during games. Engle was beloved by faculty and players for his quiet erudition and professorial approach to coaching.

"Rip was such a far cry from the coaches of today," says Edward Kiely, Paterno's center during his senior season. "Rip was so humble, he loved people and he was very compassionate. I got married at the end of my sophomore season. Rip not only came to the wedding, he got my wife a job. He was always the kind of guy who had his arm wrapped around someone's shoulder, giving them encouragement."

Engle was impressed with the way the young Paterno grasped the intellectual side of the game. By his senior year, Paterno was attending the coaches' weekly meeting, helping them assemble game plans.

"Joe was kind of on the staff," Kiely jokes.

Paterno battled senior Ed Finn and junior Walt Pastuszak for playing time at quarterback his junior year before taking control the following season.

As at Brooklyn Prep, Paterno enjoyed a big senior year at Brown, in 1949. He was elected co-captain by his teammates and played quarterback on offense and defensive back on defense.

"Joe didn't have much natural ability — his passes fluttered like knuckleballs — but his play-calling was way ahead of

[**Coach Rip Engle finds himself at the center of attention in the Brown locker room. Pulling his tie, wearing nothing but a towel, is Joe Paterno.**]

31

[**Paterno followed Engle to Penn State and became an offensive backfield coach.**]

26-6 after three quarters, but staged a fantastic comeback behind the hard running of fullback George Paterno and the adroit quarterbacking of Joe Paterno.

The only blemish on the Bears' 1949 season was a 27-14 setback at Princeton.

"I don't exactly remember the details of that game, but we should have won," Kiely insists. "We were the better football team."

In the spring of 1950, after completing his senior year, Paterno agreed to help Engle groom another quarterback to be his successor. By the end of spring drills, Engle was gone: He had accepted the head-coaching job at Penn State.

Paterno, meantime, was making plans to follow in his father's footsteps and attend law school. He applied for fall admission to Boston University's law school.

Everything appeared to be set — until Paterno received a phone call from the hills of Central Pennsylvania. It was Engle, who asked Paterno to join him as an assistant at Penn State.

Paterno, in fact, was not Engle's first choice. Engle had asked his top lieutenants at Brown, Gus Zitrides and Bill Doolittle, to join him at Penn State. But Zitrides remained at Brown when he was offered the position of head coach, and Doolittle opted to join Zitrides' staff.

Before he accepted, Paterno decided to discuss Engle's offer with his parents. His father was disappointed but gave his blessing. His mother, however, was upset.

"You didn't have to go to college to be a coach!" Paterno remembers her saying.

"I was surprised he chose coaching over law," Father Bermingham says. "Then it dawned on me: He's going to be an educator. And that's what has made him distinctive as a coach. He's affecting the lives of his players. Then it didn't surprise me anymore."

It was not exactly love at first sight when Paterno arrived in Happy Valley in the spring of 1950.

"I hated it!" Paterno says. "I was a New Yorker, a city kid, an ethnic. I went to school in the city and lived in one of the great Italian sections of any city. I was a bachelor. I wasn't there three months when I sat down with Rip and told him I was going to leave. I told him I'd stick out the football season, that this just

everyone else's," Gresh says. "He got it all from Rip. Rip saw that the game came natural to Joe."

On defense, Paterno intercepted six passes for 114 yards his senior year, boosting his career total at Brown to 14 pickoffs — still a Brown record.

Brown was one of the best teams in the East in 1949, piling up an 8-1 record. The Bears' most memorable win was a 41-26 victory over Colgate on Thanksgiving Day. The Bears trailed by

Penn State's coaching staff: front row, from left: Frank Patrick, Earl Bruce, head coach Rip Engle and Jim O'Hora. Back row, from left: Dan Radakovich, Joe McMullen, George Welsh, Joe Paterno and J.T. White. Left, a break in the action.

wasn't the place for me."

Then a funny thing happened. Paterno made friends. One of his first was Steve Suhey, a former All-America guard at Penn State, who had just moved into a two-bedroom apartment with his wife, Ginger, and their infant son. Suhey, a graduate assistant coach for Engle, rented out the second bedroom to Paterno.

After living with the Suheys for a year, Paterno took a bedroom with the family of Jim O'Hora, a retired Penn State assis-

tant. O'Hora became Paterno's best friend and confidante, offering coaching tips, career counseling and personal advice. Paterno took meals with the O'Hora family and received emotional support from them when his father unexpectedly passed away at the age of 58 in 1955.

"I guess the place grew on me," Paterno says in reflection. "The one thing that struck me about this place, that kept me

[**Paterno, left, and Steve Suhey, who shared a two-bedroom apartment along with Suhey's wife and son early in Paterno's days at Penn State.**]

around, was how loyal everyone was to it. I guess it was the inferiority complex. You know, it was a cow college. It wasn't even a university — it was Penn State College. But the alumni were so loyal to it."

What also impressed Paterno was the way the university and its faculty let him fit in and let him spread his wings.

"All this sounds so self-serving and I don't mean it to sound that way, but I could not have stayed in coaching if it was just coaching," Paterno says. "I'm too much of an intellectual snob. I'm the type of guy who likes to spout things. I like to argue with people. The environment of this place, once I got accustomed to it and met some people — I've always been allowed to do that. I was accepted by the faculty. I've been asked to do things for the university. I have to have another dimension besides coaching, and there were places where I might not have been able to do that. This place was small enough and I've kind of grown with it. So I'm very appreciative of Penn State and what it's done for me. The university has been awfully good to me."

Penn State was a good — not great — football program when Engle arrived, and it remained that way during his tenure. The Nittany Lions went 5-3-1 Engle's first year, in 1950, and 5-4 the following season. The Lions had individual stars, such as running back Lenny Moore and quarterback Milt Plum, but they made little noise on the national scene.

Engle and Penn State finally began to receive some national recognition in the late 1950's. Behind swashbuckling quarterback Richie Lucas — who was dubbed "Riverboat Richie" after a promotional photograph that depicted him as a riverboat gambler — they stunned Alabama, 7-0, in the 1959 Liberty Bowl to finish 9-2 and 11th in The Associated Press final poll. Engle completed his first decade in Happy Valley with a record of 62-28-4.

Like the Penn State football program, Paterno's personal life also was on the upswing. In the fall of 1958 he met Suzanne Pohland, a freshman from Latrobe who would become his wife.

They met, appropriately, in the library. Paterno, already pushing 32, was overseeing a study hall for football players and Sue, an 18-year-old freshman, was tutoring a player.

"He told me to keep the kid in his books, keep him in school, and then he waited for me to grow up," Sue recalls.

Because of their mutual interest in books — Sue was an English literature major — they developed a friendship. They went out for pizza or met in the library to discuss books.

"I thought of him as my buddy, my friend," says Sue, who was not a football fan. She spent most of her Saturday afternoons in the library because it was empty.

Slowly, the friendship evolved into something more.

"He was so idealistic, with lots of ideas, lots of plans. He really wanted to stay here and make it the best place he could make it," Sue says.

By the summer of 1961, they were talking marriage.

Sue had taken a job at the New Jersey shore before the start of her senior year. It was an exciting time in her life. She was already pinned to another man — sort of a pre-engagement — and had won a scholarship for graduate studies at Brown University.

Her plans changed suddenly when Paterno rented a beach house in a nearby town with his sister and her family and asked Sue to marry him. She accepted.

They then traveled to New York City to break the news to Sue's mother, who was shopping there.

Joe said he wanted to get married in two weeks, before the start of football season, but Mrs. Pohland recommended that they wait until Sue's father had a chance to speak to them.

Sue's father said he wanted her to graduate from college before she got married. Among the Pohlands' reservations was the age factor — Joe was closer in age to Sue's mother (10 years' difference) than he was to Sue (13 years).

Sue, who entered her senior year needing only eight credits, completed her undergraduate studies at Penn State in December 1961. By then, Joe was wrapped up in football. The Nittany Lions beat Georgia Tech, 30-15, in the Gator Bowl to wrap up an 8-3 season and 18th position in the final AP poll.

With recruiting season and spring practice just ahead, Joe and Sue decided to postpone their marriage plans until after completion of spring drills. They were wed on May 12, 1962, in a church in Latrobe. Their honeymoon plans, which began as a two-month trip to Europe, were eventually scaled back to five days at Virginia Beach because of monetary and other considerations. On the way to Virginia, Joe stopped to visit a football recruit in Somerset, Pa., while Sue waited in the car.

The recruit signed with Miami.

The Pohlands' concerns about Paterno subsided for a while but flared again in 1965 when Sue had the second of their five children and Joe was nowhere to be found, wrapped up in his coaching responsibilities.

Sue told her parents not to worry.

"I knew Joe was happy in his job and I knew I wanted a lot of kids, so I was happy," she says. "I didn't want to be any more liberated than I was. After a while, I think they saw we had a very solid and loving marriage, and everything was fine."

Their third child, David, was born on July 1, 1966 — the day Joe Paterno officially was recorded as head coach on the Penn State payroll, although he had accepted the position nearly five months earlier.

Paterno's coaching philosophy and techniques were borrowed from many sources, including Zev Graham and O'Hora. As a young coach, Paterno also struck up a friendship with Vince Lombardi, with whom he felt a kinship because of their Brooklyn roots and Italian heritages.

"Lombardi was a very unique person," Paterno says. "When he was a high school coach, he taught chemistry and Latin. He was a very good teacher."

By the time Paterno was at Penn State, Lombardi was known as a fiery leader and master tactician, but he couldn't get a head-coaching job.

The two men were having dinner one night in 1954 when Paterno raised the issue of why Lombardi couldn't get hired as a head coach.

"Two things," said Lombardi, who was then an assistant with the New York Giants. "I'm Catholic and I'm Italian. They're not going to hire me at a place like Virginia."

Lombardi's words haunted Paterno, who feared that his religious and ethnic heritage would hold him back in the same way. But when Engle decided to retire after the 1965 season, he pushed Paterno for the job. Paterno became Penn State's 14th

head coach on Feb. 19, 1966, one day after Engle announced his retirement and 16 years after the Italian kid from Brooklyn arrived in Happy Valley.

Many of the things the Penn State football program does today and many of the things Paterno still says were borrowed from Engle.

Lots of football teams, including Penn State, script the first dozen or so offensive plays for each game; Engle did that in the 1940's. The strong safety at Penn State is called a hero rather than a "monster," as it is at some schools, because Engle found the term inhumane.

"Joe still sprinkles his conversations with 'Rip used to say,'" says Tom Bradley, a longtime Penn State assistant.

"I think Joe has taken many things from Rip," says former Penn State Athletic Director Jim Tarman. "One thing he said that Rip would always say is, 'It's not my team; it's theirs,' meaning the players. Another of his favorites is that 'Publicity is like poison — it won't hurt you unless you swallow it.'"

Penn State's drab uniforms and Paterno's emphasis on education are reflections of Rip's beliefs, says Engle's widow, Mary (Sunny) Engle.

"It's Joe's nature, but it was Rip's, too," she says. "Rip didn't go for flash."

"I know they were close — Rip had a lot of respect for Joe," Mrs. Engle says.

If her husband were alive today to see the program, "I think he'd be delighted," says Mrs. Engle, who still lives in State College. "I think Joe has done everything for Penn State, and more. Joe has done so much not just for the football program, but for other parts of the university. Yes, I think Rip would be delighted. There are many football coaches. But there will never be another one like Joe."

[**Paterno stood by Engle's side through 16 seasons. Among the highlights: a 1959 Liberty Bowl win and a No. 11 ranking in The Associated Press poll.**]

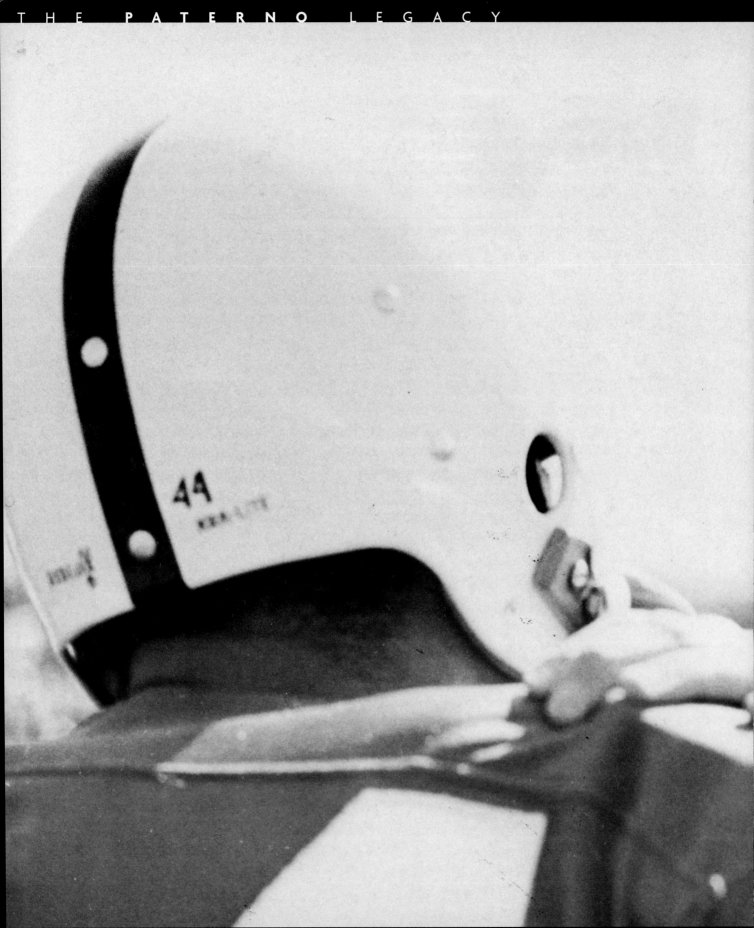

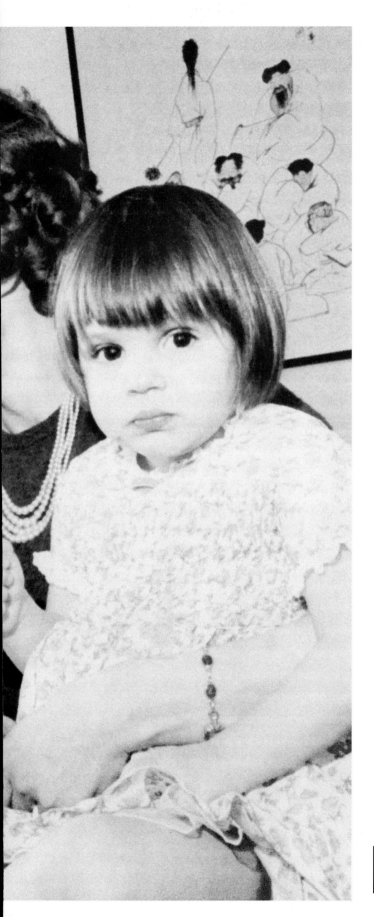

CHAPTER TWO

BY BOB SMIZIK

THE ENTIRE HISTORY of Penn State football and a major portion of the history of Penn State University and Eastern football came dangerously close to being written in a totally different script by the events that unfolded on the campus of Yale University in 1963. What we know of Penn State and its football program and the course of collegiate sports in the eastern part of the country would have never come out the way they did if it were not for a man named Johnny Pont and Yale.

Joe Paterno had been an assistant coach at Penn State for 13 years in 1963. His future was uncertain. He longed to be a head coach, but he was loath to leave Penn State. The kid from Brooklyn had found another life in Central Pennsylvania and he wasn't eager to alter it. Paterno worked for Rip Engle, a successful and popular head coach who was getting up in years. But it was not known when Engle would retire, and by no means had his successor been designated — although Paterno was certainly a candidate.

Paterno's coaching talent was becoming more widely known each year but that did not ensure a lucrative head coaching job in the immediate future. This was a different era. The turnover in coaching wasn't what it is now. Coaches weren't jumping from one job to another. The money wasn't there and neither was the prestige. The profession was more secure. Winning wasn't such an all-important quality. Character building still was in vogue.

Paterno, recently married, faced an uncertain future.

But then Yale got into the mix. The young assistant from Penn State had caught some eyes at Yale.

"One day Rip sat me down," Paterno recalled, "and said,

[**Paterno, 39, huddles at home after getting word that he would succeed Engle. On his lap is Mary Kathryn, 1. Wife Sue holds Diana Lynne, 2.**]

41

[**Among Paterno's mementos: a snapshot from his first game as Penn State's coach in 1966. That season, the Nittany Lions finished 5-5.**]

'There are very few jobs I think you ought to take. But Yale should be a good job. No. 1, you can win at Yale and if you want to go on from there, fine. But if you don't want to go on from there, the Yale alumni can make you a rich man.' "

Paterno had plans for a family. Allowing Yale alumni to make him a rich man didn't bother him. He applied for the vacancy. He didn't want to leave Penn State. But he wanted to be a head coach and if that involved leaving State College, so be it.

"I made a real try to get it," Paterno said years later. "I thought I could have done well."

By all accounts, Paterno impressed the people at Yale. But the job was not to be his — a fact Penn State can reflect on with much gratitude. Johnny Pont, coming off an undefeated season at Miami of Ohio, beat Paterno out for the job.

Joe PATERNO
• Head man at PENN STATE /

Paterno was in Philadelphia at an alumni function when Yale made the obvious phone call. If Paterno was a viable candidate two years earlier, he would be an even better one now.

"I got a message to call Delaney Kipphuth," the athletic director, he said. "I knew Pont had left and I figured they wanted me to come up for another interview. But they offered me the job on the phone. I told them I had to have time to think about it."

He wasn't getting any younger, and this was an offer from one of the finest academic institutions in the world. Ivy League football, although in decline, had not yet reached the point where it is today. The offer was intriguing.

He went to his mentor.

"I came back to State College and I said to Rip, 'What do you think?'

"He said, 'Joe, I don't know whether you should take that job unless you want to leave Penn State.'

"They told me they were giving the job to Pont because it was late and he could bring his whole staff with him," Paterno said.

History tells us that Paterno never did leave Penn State, that he eventually became head coach, that he turned a good program into a great one, that the school's emergence from cow college to major university was aided by the might and prestige of this football program and that along the way the coach became a legend.

But Pont isn't ready to exit this drama just yet.

He lasted only two seasons at Yale before leaving for Indiana. He had bigger plans than the Ivy League. He wanted to get rich on his own, not to be made so by the Yale alumni. And just as Pont's arrival at Yale had prevented Paterno from leaving Penn State in 1963, now his departure from that school would not only ensure Paterno's staying but he would pave the way for his promotion.

JOE PATERNO
BROWN '50
SUCCEEDS RIP ENGLE
AS HEAD FOOTBALL COACH
AT PENN STATE

HE HAS BEEN RIP'S ASSISTANT
SINCE GRADUATION. QUARTERBACK
AND CO-CAPTAIN OF ENGLE'S LAST BROWN
TEAM, WHICH POSTED AN 8-1-0 RECORD

"I told him all I ever wanted to do was be the head coach at Penn State. But you tell me I ought to look at it, I figure . . . whatever you tell me to do, I'll do."

Eventually, Engle told Paterno, "I'm going to leave soon. I think you can get this job."

But that wasn't assurance enough for Paterno. He had reason to be leery. He had watched the coming of age of one of the greatest coaches in the history of football and seen the difficulty that man had encountered in achieving his dream. Paterno had known Vince Lombardi since he was a child. They grew up in the same Brooklyn neighborhood. Paterno had played ball against Lombardi's younger brother. The two had stayed in touch in coaching and Paterno followed Lombardi's career closely. By now Lombardi was coaching the Green Bay

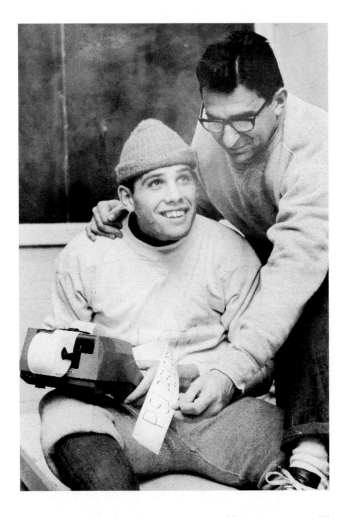

[**Quarterback Tom Sherman was able to ring up some victories for Paterno during the following year, 1967, when PSU went 8-2-1.**]

Packers, but Paterno knew the long path Lombardi had taken to get that job. He had been struck by the difficulty Lombardi, acknowledged by almost everyone as a superior coach, had in securing a head job.

"When Lombardi was an assistant with the Giants he would come up to the campus," Paterno says. "I'd go out to dinner with him. He had been on the Army staff with Earl Blaik and Blaik had said he was the best assistant he ever had. But he never got a head job. He was supposed to get the Fordham job and they gave it to someone else. Jobs were filled at Wake Forest and Minnesota and Virginia where he had applied. Those guys got jobs and he didn't. I didn't understand it."

Lombardi's explanation — "Two things. I'm Catholic and I'm Italian" — gave Paterno pause. He was Catholic like Lombardi and had the distinctive look of an Italian about him.

So when Engle said he thought he could get Paterno the Penn State job, Paterno wasn't convinced. Lombardi's history was fresh in his mind.

"I said, 'Coach, that's fine. But will the president give me this job? Will he get me past the board of trustees?' "

Engle had a simple answer. "Let's go talk to Eric Walker."

Walker was the Penn State president.

"Eric was one of those guys who gave you 15 minutes and that's it," Paterno says. "Eric said, 'What are you here for?'

"I told him I was concerned about whether I could get this job. He said, 'If you're good enough, you'll get the job.'

"I said, 'I'm good enough, that's not the problem.' I mentioned the things Lombardi had said. He started to laugh."

"We just opened a research lab in Italy. You know why? Because I like Italians."

That was enough for Paterno. Penn State's next coach was waiting in line.

"I called Delaney [at Yale] and told him I wasn't going to take the job. Rip made me associate head coach after that."

Had Paterno not received assurances that he would succeed Engle, there's no telling in what direction he might have gone. But if it had been to Yale, it might have been for a long time. Carm Cozza, the man who eventually succeeded Pont, coached from 1965 through 1996.

Engle retired after the 1965 season. He left Paterno a 5-5 team and, as the joke goes, not wishing to show any disrespect, Paterno brought back his first team at 5-5.

But it was no joke to Paterno. His well-known competitive drive wasn't developed after his teams got good. "I wasn't sure then how good I could be as a head coach," Paterno says. "But I was darn sure I'd find out pretty quick, not stagger around for four or five years. I'd made up my mind in a hurry about that."

The Lions lost three of their first five games — 42-8 at Michigan State, 11-0 at Army and 49-11 at UCLA. Against UCLA, Bruins coach Tommy Prothro used an onside kick late in the game with his team leading by a large margin. Penn State wasn't expecting it, UCLA recovered and went in for another score.

"We felt like naked jerks 2,500 miles from home," Paterno was to say, "and I the exposed head jerk."

The Lions lost by two to Syracuse and were shut out, 21-0, by Georgia Tech later in the season.

Paterno was beginning to doubt himself and the doubts reached a crescendo when the Lions opened the next season with a 23-22 loss at Navy. It wasn't just a loss, it was how it happened.

Bobby Campbell's touchdown run had given the Lions a 22-17 lead with less than two minutes remaining. There was understandable jubilation on the Penn State side of the field. It was short-lived. Navy quarterback John Cartwright needed only about a minute to pass his team to victory. That Cartwright would have his way so easily against the Lions was not a surprise. For the game, the Navy offense amassed 489 yards.

Paterno was one game into his second season and he was a less-than-.500 coach. This was not what he expected upon entering the profession. The young coach had come to one of the first crossroads of his career.

[**Tom Sherman and Paterno discuss strategy on Penn State's sideline. Sherman was a three-time letterman and a team co-captain.**]

47

"Here we were, 5-6 in my first 11 games. Our staff was confused and needed strong leadership. I had to either prove myself or, well, there was no use prolonging it.

"I got on the bus [from Navy] knowing we were 5-6 and we were lousy. It wasn't like we had played well or we were coached well. That would have been one thing. But we were lousy. We weren't that bad my first year. We got licked by Syracuse, which had [Larry] Csonka. We got licked by Georgia Tech, which played in the Sugar Bowl. We got licked by Michigan State and we got licked by UCLA, which played in the Rose Bowl. So four of those five games, I felt, 'Well, that's OK.' "

But snatching defeat from the jaws of victory against Navy was not OK.

"I got home and I said to Sue, 'I don't know if I'm a head coach and I better find out pretty damn quick. I'm going to play some different people.' That's when I started to play Ham and Smear and Reid and Onkotz and those guys."

The next game was the turning point. It was at Miami and Paterno was determined to do it his way, as unusual as that way might have to be. It showed, if nothing else, the resourcefulness of the coach and how far he was willing to reach to succeed.

"We played on a Saturday night in Miami. We left Penn State to go to Pittsburgh on Friday. We worked out at Moon Township High School and stayed at the old Greater Pittsburgh Airport that night. The hotel there was air-conditioned. It's the third Saturday in September and it was hot. We landed in Miami, where the airport is air-conditioned, put them on an air-conditioned bus. We went to an air-conditioned motel. When we got to the Orange Bowl that night we gave them only a 15 minute warmup. They never had a chance to learn how hot it was.

"When we won that one, I started to feel a lot better about coaching."

And if Penn State hadn't defeated Miami, how would Paterno have felt about his coaching future?

"I had kids to bring up. I didn't want to be a 42-year-old guy out of a job. If we had not beaten Miami or played well, I probably would have sat down with some people and said,

'Hey, you better starting looking around.' "

And what about Paterno's future?

"If I could have swung it, I would have gone to law school. Sue and I had talked about it. We would have figured something out."

As it turns out, all that had to be figured was how to handle one of the greatest runs in coaching history, a run that established Penn State and Paterno, a run that paved the way for future greatness.

There was a sidelight to that Miami victory that could have become a lowlight except Paterno made it a highlight.

While the team was waiting to board its flight back to Pennsylvania, Paterno spotted two players — both regulars — in an airport bar, each with a beer. The rules about drinking had been made totally clear to the players previously. What these two were doing was in direct violation of a team rule.

One of the players had previously been in trouble with the police. Addressing him, Paterno said, "You're gone." He was off the team. The other player, because Paterno knew of no previous trouble, was suspended for two games.

That was hardly the end of the incident.

On Monday night, the team captains, Tom Sherman and Bill Lenkaitis, paid a visit to their coach. They told Paterno the team was meeting at that moment and had sent the captains to express their belief that the punishment for the two players was too harsh. They wanted the one player back on the team and the suspension removed from the other player. What was more, they wanted Paterno's decision immediately.

Paterno told the captains to go back to the meeting and he would follow them shortly.

When Paterno addressed the team, he said, "A rule that protects us all was broken. The decision I made was the best one for all of us. I have no choice but to stand with it. If anybody here can't live with it, go. Right now. If you stay, you do it my way, the right way, living by the rules. If you decide to

[**Paterno's first two seasons as head coach were at times tumultuous. Soon enough, he made his mark as a disciplinarian and as a winner.**]

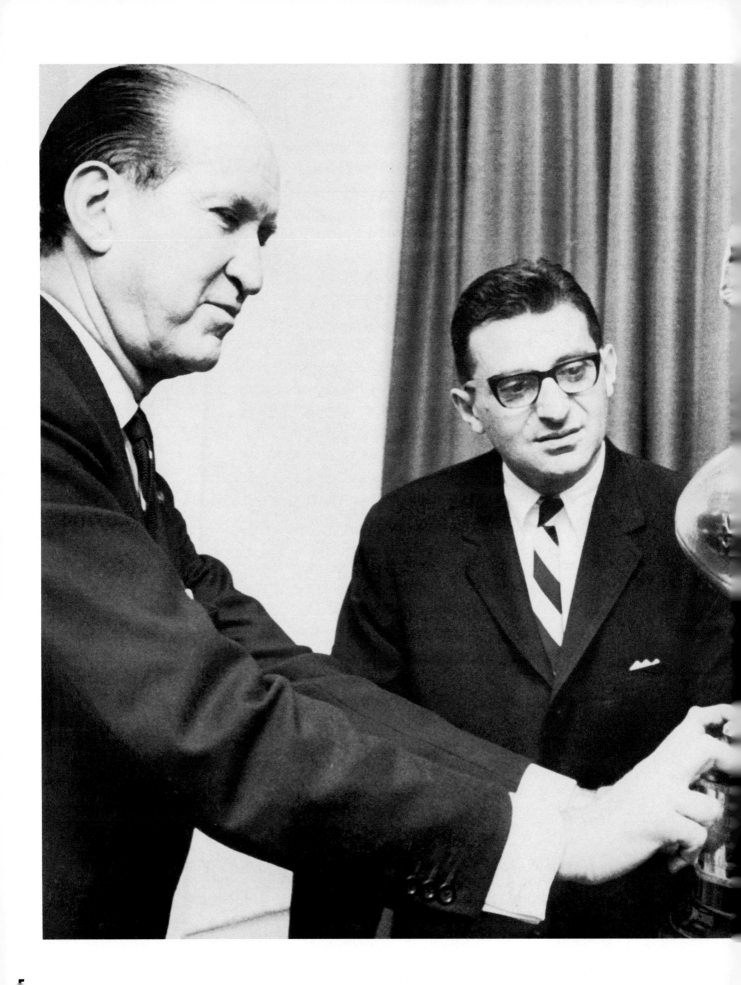

Dec. 14, 1967: In New York, Henry L. Lambert, presents the Lambert Trophy to Joe Paterno and co-captains Bill Lenkaitis and Jim Litterelle.

stay and do it that way, we'll have a great football team. I'm going to walk out of here right now. A minute later I'm coming back in. Whoever's here, that's who we're going to play with."

When Paterno returned 60 seconds later no one had left. Not all of them were happy, but they were there ready to conduct themselves under the rules established by the coach.

The victory against Miami was no less important to the future of the Penn State program than the lesson the players learned in its aftermath.

The Lions lost the following week, to third-ranked UCLA, but even in defeat there was reason for optimism. UCLA had defeated Penn State by 38 points the previous year. This season it was by two. And then came the deluge.

What followed was what amounted to the birth of Penn State football as it is known today. The Lions didn't lose again until Sept. 26, 1970 — a period in which they were 30-0-1. They won with some of the greatest defensive teams in college football history. They won with brilliant offensive performers. They won with class and they won with dignity. Paterno was determined to do it his way, and he did. The greatness of the program was established during the 1968 and 1969 seasons. The Lions were 22-0 and grasped the attention of the nation, if not the pollsters. They didn't win a national championship during that span, but they established Eastern football as a force and Penn State football as something more. Included in all of that was the rise of Paterno. He was no longer the hot young assistant. He was fast becoming a giant of the game, a man who could win and win the right way.

And he had a plan for how it should be done, a plan different from the typical college program.

"Maybe that winning season [1967] came too quickly and suddenly," he said in his book, "Paterno: By the Book." "Maybe I had the heady idea I had conquered the secrets of winning at football. Maybe I already felt that winning for its own sake left a certain emptiness. Whatever the root of it, some unsatisfied itch in me required looking ahead to a next challenge, maybe something bigger that seemed more significant.

"Something made me itch toward a different kind of goal — not football that puts winning first, but first-class football played by students who put first-class lives first. Maybe I wanted to recreate at this more-or-less ordinary state university, for these kids of more-or-less ordinary farm and working-class family backgrounds, something like the excitement that made most days at Brown University wonderful for me.

"I keep saying 'maybe' because I can't clearly recall how the dream was formed."

In a column by Bill Conlin, a Philadelphia sports writer, Paterno more clearly defined his dream and for the first time gave it a name — The Grand Experiment.

"I'm thinking in terms of a Grand Experiment. It sounds a little corny, I know, but it's that kind of thing for us because we intend doing it with people who belong at Penn State. Everybody assumes if you have a great football team there have to be sacrifices in the area of [academic] standards. People tell me it can't be done without sacrificing standards. They tell me I'm daydreaming."

We want "to play football in the best league possible, with people who belong in college, and who kept things in perspective. Look, I want these kids to enjoy football. But I also want them to enjoy college. I want them to learn art and literature and music and all the other things college has to offer. There's room for it. Colleges should be a great time. It's the only time a person is really free. I don't want my players just tied to a football program."

"Joe had a dream back then," says Ernie Accorsi, who worked in the sports information office in 1969 and 1970 and later went on to become general manager of the Cleveland Browns. "He set such high standards. He said we can be like Texas and Michigan and Notre Dame. I grew up 80 miles away," in Hershey, "and I never believed that could happen.

"That's why I have so much personal respect for the man, because of what he created. I didn't even graduate from there but I go back almost every year since I've left. It's almost like going back to a retreat. I feel an infusion of inspiration."

Few realized the greatness and the disappointment that were to follow when Penn State opened the 1968 season with a 31-6 win over Navy. The victory showed how much the Lions had improved from the previous year, when they lost to Navy,

and how much room for growth there was at University Park. The crowd at Beaver Stadium for the Navy game was 49,273 — then the third largest in history. Today, the people at that game would barely fill half of the expanded Beaver Stadium.

When Penn State defeated Kansas State the following week, the Lions were ranked fourth in the nation. Paterno was asked about the significance of polls.

"A political poll represents a reflection of public sentiment, but football polls are little more than calculated guesses," he said. "Very seldom do they end the way they started. They do create interest, but serve no purpose as far as the outcome of the season is concerned."

Charlie Pittman, a superb running back, and Ted Kwalick, an early edition of the prototype tight end that would come to be such a factor in both the college and pro games, were the headliners on offense. But the key was quarterback Chuck Burkhart, a player of modest talent who rarely made mistakes, never rattled and rose to the occasion when necessary.

When Paterno was quarterbacking Brown, the great New York newspaperman Stanley Woodward described him as a quarterback who "can't run, can't pass — just thinks and wins." If Woodward had covered Burkhart, he might have used those words a second time.

"Sure, he might look bad at times," Paterno said of Burkhart, "but he has the ability to come up with the big plays. He never knows when he's licked."

But defense drove this team, and what a defense it was — Mike Reid, Jack Ham, Steve Smear, Dennis Onkotz, Jim Kates and Neal Smith. It was relentless in halting the opposition, incredible in being able to manufacture big plays.

The Lions rolled through the season, winning by an average of 23 points a game and impressing almost everyone but the pollsters. The East had little respect at the time. The Big 10, Southeastern, Big Eight, Southwest and Pac-10 got most of the respect.

[**Paterno goes over his game plan for the 1967 Gator Bowl, pitting Penn State and Florida State, in Jacksonville. The game ended in a 17-17 tie.**]

"People weren't even sure who Penn State was," Ham says. "A lot of times Penn State was being confused with the University of Pennsylvania. In a lot of people's minds, the Ivy League was Eastern football.

"That was one of Joe's big things — to get respect for Eastern football. He was the guy out front talking about how good Eastern football was."

The Lions were invited to the Orange Bowl where the opponent would be Kansas, champion of the Big Eight. The result was an excellent game with a bizarre, stranger-than-fiction ending that established the meeting as one of the most memorable football games in the history of both schools and of the Orange Bowl.

Kansas led, 14-7, with about two minutes remaining. If the Jayhawks got a first down, the game probably would have

Following the 1967 Gator Bowl, Joe and Sue Paterno take a well-deserved nap aboard the plane as they ride back to State College.

been over. But this was the day of the big play. Reid broke through to dump a Kansas ball carrier for a 13-yard loss. When Kansas punted, the Lions came after Bill Bell with 10 men. The strategy worked. Smith got a piece of the ball and it rolled dead on the Penn State 49.

It was the biggest game of his life, but Paterno remained calm on the sideline.

"We had two timeouts left and really plenty of time to win the ball game — if we had any kind of offense. Kansas was the one under the gun. We had Campbell and Kwalick, two great receivers."

Paterno's plan was to lull Kansas into thinking he had panicked. He discussed his strategy on the sideline with Burkhart and Campbell. Turns out, though, Burkhart and Campbell had a strategy of their own.

"Kansas would be looking for a short pass," Paterno said. "They thought we'd be playing it safe and careful and that's what I wanted them to think. But I said to Bobby, 'You run a deep post pattern, run for the goal post. Chuck, you go back and just throw the ball out of the end zone. I'm not interested in completing a pass here. They'll think we're desperate or stupid, but then we'll throw a short one to Kwalick.'

"Next play, delay Kwalick, let everybody clear out and dump him a short one. I knew if he got the ball in an open field he could run over everybody and at least get it in there deep. So that was my plan. Even if Ted made only 15 or 20 yards, we'd be down in there and then they'd have a lot to worry about.

"I thought this was pretty good strategy, but I'm not sure Chuck and Bobby were even listening to me. I heard Bobby say to Chuck, 'I'm going to be at the left goal post. The ball better be there.' And Chuck answered, 'Don't worry, it'll be there.' I yelled at them, 'Don't even try to complete it. Get it out of bounds, no interception.' "

Paterno was correct. They weren't listening to him. Campbell beat two Kansas defenders deep and was tackled on the 3-yard line.

Paterno called a three-play series. The first two had fullback Tom Cherry hitting the middle of the line. If that didn't produce a touchdown, he would send in a play. Cherry got nothing and Paterno called for an inside handoff to Pittman — the scissors play.

But again Burkhart, the apple of the coach's eye, disregarded his instructions. He sensed that the play wouldn't work, that the Kansas defense was primed to stop Pittman. Burkhart did the unthinkable. He didn't handoff to the team's best running back. He decided to try to take it in himself — he, a player who had never scored a touchdown on the college level.

The "fake" surprised everyone.

"For an awful moment, I thought I had missed the handoff," Pittman said. "Then I was piled up. I looked over and Chuck was scoring."

The Lions trailed by a point and everyone knew Paterno would go for two and the win. There was no overtime in college football and a tie appealed to no one.

Paterno called for a pass and Burkhart lobbed the ball high into the end zone toward Kwalick. But he was well covered and the ball was batted away.

Even though time remained, Kansas supporters stormed the field. They never saw the flag thrown by umpire Foster Grose. The Jayhawks had too many men on the field. The Lions would get another try.

Paterno's "Grand Experiment" was to produce a successful football program without sacrificing its academic integrity.

Paterno called for a quick pitch right to Campbell. When Burkhart brought the team to the line, there was so much noise he asked for quiet and was allowed to take the team back to a huddle. Now Paterno had second thoughts. His original call had been geared to stay away from John Zook, the Jayhawks' All-America defensive end. But given more time, Paterno realized Zook had been the easier of the two Kansas ends to block. He called for Campbell to take a handoff and sweep left. Charlie Zapiec, another player from this team to become an All-America, got just enough of Zook to let Campbell squeeze by and into the end zone.

The wildest ending imaginable for a football game and the Lions were halfway through two of the most spectacular seasons in college football history.

Penn State had waited 56 years between undefeated and untied seasons. How could it expect another the very next year? But, in fact, how could it not? There was greatness almost everywhere on this team. To be sure, hopes were higher than the season before. This time those hopes came with the alarming baggage known as national championship aspirations.

It is well known by now that Penn State did not win a national title in 1969, although it went undefeated again and again had a corps of players that had to be the equal of any in the nation.

Not that the Lions were ignored that season, not that their accomplishments were not known across the land. This Penn State team was so good that it took the President of the United States to step in and NOT declare it national champion.

Richard Nixon didn't get involved until late in the season, and when he did Paterno stood in there with the President, showing for the first — but hardly the last — time that his statesmanship was almost as brilliant as his coaching.

Although at this point in his career, Paterno's stature was hardly what it was years later.

Accorsi remembers a trip to Philadelphia with Paterno in the summer of 1969.

"We had a meeting at one of the television stations about our highlights film," Accorsi recalled. "We got there

Penn State won the 1969 Orange Bowl, 15-14, and returned the following year to beat Missouri. Right, Paterno and Missouri Coach Dan Devine.

early and we went to the lounge of The Warwick Hotel to kill some time. The bartender looked at Joe and said, 'I know you, but I can't place you. You coach in this town, don't you?'

"Joe said no. Then the guy said, 'Your name is Frank Petrini.'

"We left and Joe laughed. 'Can you image Bear Bryant walking into a bar in Birmingham and no one knowing who he was?'

"It was that way with the team. We didn't get the respect the other teams did. We were always the lowest ranked of the undefeated teams. They made fun of our schedule. They didn't believe we were that good."

The season was not without its difficult moments. The Lions traveled to Manhattan, Kan., on Oct. 4 to take on a talented Kansas State team that was ranked 20th in the nation. They took a 17-0 lead and won, 17-14, as the Wildcats scored late against reserves. It was a good win, but didn't impress the people voting in the polls.

The Lions were 4-0 on Oct. 18 when they went to Syracuse. They came very close to coming away 4-1. Syracuse led, 14-0, at the half.

"I never saw a Penn State team so bewildered," Paterno said of the first half. "Syracuse was making all the big plays. It was all turned around. We looked like Syracuse and Syracuse looked like Penn State."

At halftime, Paterno talked to the players of defeat, how if they tried hard the rest of the way they could still hold their heads up. He said, "We've won with class, let's lose with class."

It was the ultimate Paterno, a desperate grasp for desperate times. And it worked — even if the players didn't realize it — as the Lions came back for a 15-14 victory.

Years later, Lydell Mitchell, the great running back, spoke of the game with Accorsi when both were with the Baltimore Colts. "That was the only time I was disappointed in him," Mitchell said of Paterno's halftime talk. "He quit on us."

Accorsi looked at Mitchell in slight bewilderment and said, "He didn't quit on you. You won the game. There was a method to what he did."

The Lions won the remainder of their games by at least 20 points, which meant, although neither knew it at the time, that Paterno and Nixon were on a collision course.

Paterno figured his team had no chance to play for No. 1 because Ohio State had that ranking and it was tied into the Rose Bowl and would play the Pac-10 champ. Since No. 1 seemed out of the question, Paterno threw open the matter of which bowl the team should attend to his players.

He discussed the topic thoroughly in his autobiography, *Paterno: By the Book.*

"I wanted the experienced kids on our team to vote on where we would go. First, I called in some of the black players — Lydell Mitchell, Charlie Pittman, Franco Harris and a few others. This was at the peak of the new civil rights awareness and I wanted to hear them out first about any choice among Southern cities. They didn't want to go to the Cotton Bowl," where the opponent would be Texas or Arkansas. "More specifically, they didn't want to go to

Paterno's legacy includes putting his school on the map. "People weren't even sure who Penn State was," says a former star, Jack Ham.

Dallas, where John F. Kennedy had been shot.

"The revulsion seemed particularly strong among young black people who linked gun-loving Dallas with the lingering racism that had once been taken for granted throughout the South. The other players seemed sensitive to what their black teammates wanted."

In a vote conducted six days before the bowl pairings were announced, the Penn State players decided overwhelmingly to go to the Orange Bowl, where they had had a great time and a great game the year before, and face Missouri, regarded as the best offensive team in the country.

The issue became more complicated when on the day of the bowl pairing announcement, in a stunning upset, Michigan beat Ohio State. That meant a Penn State-Texas game in the Cotton Bowl would have been for the national championship.

But Texas still had to play Arkansas, an excellent team but

Paterno coached the East stars in the 1969 Coaches All-America game. At practice, he explains a play to Buster O'Brien of Richmond.

one that already had been beaten.

Enter Bud Wilkinson, the former Oklahoma coach, a commentator for ABC and a friend of President Nixon. Wilkinson announced that the Texas-Arkansas game would be for the national title. Not surprisingly, the game was being carried by ABC.

To make certain no one took his pronouncement lightly, Wilkinson got Nixon to attend the game and present a No. 1 trophy to the winner.

And, sure enough, there was Nixon in the Texas locker room after the victory over Arkansas proclaiming the Longhorns to be No. 1.

Nixon was too smart a politician to ignore Pennsylvania and Penn State. At the same time he announced he would present a plaque to Penn State for having the longest winning streak in the country. Not exactly much of a consolation prize.

Paterno did not shrink from the national stage, nor from taking on a President.

In a written statement, he said, "Although I have heard nothing about a President's plaque, it would be a disservice to our squad, to Pennsylvania and to the East to accept such an award, and perhaps, to Missouri, which just might be the nation's best team. Because I had to baby-sit during the Texas-Arkansas game, I missed the President's final remarks, but it would seem a waste of his very valuable time to present Penn State with a plaque for something we already have undisputed possession of — the nation's longest winning and unbeaten streaks."

If there was any doubt as to the Lions' excellence, it ended in the Orange Bowl. The players seemed determined to let the country know exactly how great they were. The Missouri offense was silenced. The Tigers had been averaging 36 points and 450 yards a game. They got three points and 175 yards in a 10-3 defeat. The great receiver Mel Gray was held without a catch. Quarterback Terry McMillan was intercepted seven times.

The Penn State front four of Reid, Smear, John Ebersole and Gary Hull was relentless. Missouri never had a chance.

"I've never seen a defense like Penn State's," McMillan said. "They always rushed four men and forced me to throw before I was ready. Seven men were in their pass coverage. They covered my men like blankets. I threw a few passes away to avoid interceptions at first, but when we got behind I had to try to hit, but heck, the receivers were always covered. I never even saw Mel Gray once."

Texas went on to play Notre Dame in the Cotton Bowl and won. The pollsters voted the Longhorns first and Penn State second.

One of the greatest teams in college football history and perhaps the greatest defense ever had been overlooked for a second straight season. But in the 1960's and 1970's, the religion of "We're No. 1," had not taken hold in America. It was still a time when winning wasn't everything.

"It wasn't as big back then as it is now," says Ham. "You play the cards that were dealt you. What else can you do?"

Almost 30 years later, Paterno would not back away from the greatness of that team.

"To this day, I don't think anybody in the country could have beaten us," he said. And as if to give that comment a little more weight, he added, "I don't say that about the 1994 team," which, of course, was another undefeated and uncrowned Penn State team.

The winning streak ended emphatically the second week of the 1970 season on a trip to Colorado where the Lions were routed by the Buffaloes, 41-13. The graduation losses had been staggering, but the Lions still had a multitude of talented players and the margin of defeat was unexpected.

When the team returned home at 3:30 a.m. the next day, Paterno addressed a crowd of about 2,000 students.

"We've come home from many trips during the last three years when it's been easy for us to come back and easy for you to come out here and meet us. We appreciate it deeply. We've won a lot of games during the past few seasons and we've always tried to be gracious winners. Now I hope we can be gracious losers. We've had many moments of glory and I'm sure we'll share many more such moments in the future. But

right now we must regenerate ourselves, and we'll need your support, the kind of support you've shown us this morning."

But it would get worse before it got better. The Lions went to Wisconsin the following week and lost, 29-16. Two weeks later, in front of a Homecoming crowd, they lost to Syracuse, 24-7.

Penn State, which had gone almost three seasons without defeat, all of a sudden had lost three times in five games.

Paterno was never one to stand idly by and accept defeat. Mike Cooper had been the starting quarterback, a position he partially earned by backing up Burkhart for two seasons. Cooper was black in an era when black quarterbacks were extremely rare. It was a tough decision for Paterno and racists frequently called his home with ugly comments. But after a 2-3 start and the prospect of a losing season, Paterno had to make a move. He bypassed backup Bob Parsons, who also had not been impressive over the first five games, and went to sophomore John Hufnagel.

Incredibly, Hufnagel came from the same Western Pennsylvania high school of Montour that had produced Burkhart. And more incredibly, the team responded to Hufnagel as it had to Burkhart. His stats were minimal that season, but with Pittman, Mitchell and Harris to carry the ball, passing wasn't all that important.

The Lions won their final five games and began another winning streak which stretched until the 11th game of the next season, when they lost to Tennessee.

By now, Hufnagel had come into his own — he threw for over 3,000 yards in his final two seasons — and the Lions were again a major force. They finished fifth in the nation in 1971 with their 11-1 record and got some sweet redemption in their bowl game.

That season they did go to the Cotton Bowl, they did play Texas and they responded with a 30-6 whipping of the Longhorns.

After his first season, the Lions were 48-6-1 over the next five. The Grand Experiment was rolling and Joe Paterno was on his way to a greatness not even his staunchest admirers could expect.

CHAPTER THREE

BY LORI SHONTZ

AS OMENS for a marriage go, Joe Paterno's first meeting with his mother-in-law was not, by any means, a good one.

He drove her to drink.

Alma Pohland was not a drinker. But she agreed to meet her daughter, Sue, in the bar of New York's famous Astor Hotel one summer afternoon. Sue said she had important news to discuss.

Alma figured Sue would announce she was engaged to the nice young man whose fraternity pin she had worn for the past year. But Sue walked into the bar not with the fraternity man, but with a man 13 years her senior. She introduced him as Joe Paterno, an assistant football coach at Penn State, where Sue was getting ready to start her senior year.

Joe asked Mrs. Pohland if she wanted a drink. Mrs. Pohland, who rarely touched alcohol, said no. Then Sue explained that she and Joe were getting married in two weeks, because Joe wanted to have everything settled before football season started again.

Alma Pohland took a deep breath and said, "I think I'll have a whiskey sour."

Then she downed it.

But from such a beginning came a perfect match.

In 35 years of marriage, Sue and Joe have raised five children, all successful in their chosen fields, and they're now enjoying their rules as Grandma and Grandpa of two little boys and a little girl.

Centre Daily Times

Date: February 28, 1962

—Bill Coleman
FUTURE BRIDE: The engagement of Suzanne Pohland, daughter of Mr. and Mrs. August L. Pohland of Latrobe to Joseph V. Paterno of State College, son of Mrs. Florence Paterno of Brooklyn, N. Y., and the late A. L. Paterno, has been announced by her parents. A spring wedding is being planned.

[**Joe and Sue Paterno exchanged wedding vows on May 12, 1962.**]

And along the way, they have become role models for the entire Penn State community.

It was a long road for Joe, who when he arrived at Penn State in 1950, was too wrapped up in football to bother setting up his own household. Coach Rip Engle and his wife offered Joe a room in their house. He took it. Several months later, when former Penn State All-America Steve Suhey moved back to town, Suhey and his wife, Ginger (daughter of former Penn State coach Bob Huggins) offered to rent their second bedroom to Joe.

After a year with the Suheys, Joe rented a room from assistant coach Jim O'Hora and his wife, Betts. He stayed with them for nine years, through the lightning strike that demolished his third-story room, the O'Horas' move to a bigger home and the way Joe threw his spaghetti and meatballs against the wall to see if they were done.

In 1961, 11 years after he arrived in State College, Jim O'Hora gave Joe a little lecture, and Joe got his own apartment. "When Jim gave me that little speech," Paterno wrote in his autobiography, *Paterno: By the Book,* "I had already met Suzanne Pohland, so it's not absolutely true that if not for Jim O'Hora's eviction notice I'd still be single."

As Penn State's only bachelor coach, Joe was assigned to monitor the team's study hall, which was held in Pattee Library. He met Suzanne Pohland, a freshman, because she was tutoring one of the football players. He told her later

than he had decided almost immediately that he would marry her someday. Says Sue, "He waited for me to grow up."

While he waited, Sue dated several other men. Joe was simply a friend, a guy she met for pizza or talked literature with. "It wasn't a date," Sue stresses.

The summer after her sophomore year, Sue took a job waitressing at a hotel in Avon by the Sea, at the New Jersey shore. Joe rented a beach house in a neighboring town; his mother and sister spent much of the summer there, and he

stopped by when his job permitted. And of course he stopped by to see Sue.

One afternoon, Sue got a call from Joe, saying he was in town and wanted to get a pizza that night. She said she had a date. "I'm only here for one night," Joe said. So Sue told her date she had to be home by 9 o'clock because she had to spend time with a friend who was just in town for the day. Her date accused her of two-timing him. Answered Sue, "You stay and watch. He's older — not a boyfriend, not a date."

Off the field, Joe and Sue coached a wonderful family. Their first two children were girls — Diana and Mary Kay. Three boys — David, Jay and Scott — came shortly thereafter.

Then Joe tried to turn himself into a date. After pizza, he tried to kiss Sue.

"I hit him and left," Sue says. "I didn't hear from him for a long time."

But several months later, when both were back on campus, Joe called Sue, and once again they became pizza buddies. And when she returned to the shore to waitress after her junior year, he followed, this time spending the entire summer in his rented beach house.

Sue served breakfast from 8 a.m. to 11 a.m. and dinner from 6 p.m. until close. She spent most of her afternoons on the beach, reading. Joe would meet her there and read, too.

One afternoon, she said she had to leave early because her boyfriend, the guy she was pinned to, was coming to visit. She and Joe argued; he said, "You're not in love with him."

The argument made Sue think. She quarreled with her boyfriend, too, and at the end of the evening she gave his pin back.

Then Joe didn't call for almost a week. "The smartest thing he ever did," Sue says, laughing.

When Joe finally did call, six days later, he asked Sue to marry him. Sue said yes, and they decided to get married in two weeks, before football season started. That's why they made arrangements to meet Sue's mother; to tell her about the wedding.

Alma Pohland always spent some time each summer in New York, shopping and seeing Broadway plays. "On this trip, I ruined her R and R," Sue says, laughing again.

With the news, Sue's father quickly joined them in New

The Paternos' vacation on Nantucket in 1975.

A walk in the woods for the family of seven.

[Joe's 200th win is one that takes the cake.]

[On a Nike trip, Joe takes time out to do the limbo.]

◖   **Christmas brings a PSU-blue sweater for Sue.**   ◗

York. He suggested that the couple wait until the end of the school year so they would have more time to plan a wedding. Unsaid was her parents' belief that Joe was probably too old for her.

So Joe returned to Penn State and coached. Sue returned to Penn State and finished her senior year. She turned down a scholarship at Brown and instead did her student teaching at Baldwin High School, in a southern suburb of Pittsburgh.

Joe and Sue were married on May 12, 1962. Says Sue, "I had no idea what I was getting into."

She found out quickly. Their honeymoon plans went from two months in Europe to two weeks in Bermuda to five days in Virginia Beach. And on the way, Joe stopped to visit a player he was trying to recruit.

"He told me it wouldn't be dull," Sue says. "You grow with it."

Joe and Sue grew into a dynamic team. "We're pretty much alike," Sue says. "Except I'm handy at repairing things,

A trip to Pittsburgh includes a Pirates game.

David, Sue, Mary Kay, Diana, Joe, Scott and Jay.

Even Joe's pajamas show off his ankles.

Diana shows school spirit with Dad in 1978.

Joe and sister Florence celebrate Mom's birthday.

*The President and Mrs. Reagan
request the pleasure of the company of
Mr. and Mrs. Paterno
at dinner
on Tuesday, March 31, 1987
at 7:30 o'clock*

Black Tie

Joe and Sue are no strangers to the White House. Below, at a 1987 state dinner in honor of Prime Minister and Mrs. Chirac of France. Right, another visit to meet President Reagan.

To Suzanne Pa
With best wis

Ronald Reagan

and he's not."

In addition to home repairs, Sue taught English and drama at Bellefonte High School until the birth of their first child, Diana, in 1963. Then she stayed at home and raised Diana, Mary Kay, David, Jay and Scott. The family moved into a home at the end of McKee Drive in the College Heights section of State College in 1969, when Jay was 10 months old. They've lived there ever since.

Joe got as involved with his kids as his job allowed.

Recruiting, especially, kept him on the road. The kids missed their father, so Sue devised a system so they'd know when he was coming back. She tied a string to the bed of the youngest child, and every night at bedtime, that child would slide a bead to the other end of the string. Then everyone would know how many "sleeps" until Dad came back.

At first, Joe tried to attend his children's activities, but he discovered that he was too recognizable. He tried to watch Diana cheer, Mary Kay do gymnastics, Jay play football and Scott play ice hockey, but each time he was hounded by autograph seekers and went home so he wouldn't take away from the game.

The kids adjusted, too. They introduced themselves by their first names only, never adding their last. Sue does the same thing; when someone sees her credit card or something and asks, "Are you related to Joe Paterno?" she answers, "Only by marriage."

That ruse used to work in State College. Now it works better the farther from home she gets.

Eating in restaurants was a problem, too. At first, the Paternos simply didn't have enough money for a family of seven to go out often. Then, they were too easily recognized. To this day, Joe and Sue rarely eat anywhere but at home.

So the family had fun there. They played cards; Joe

> **The Paternos at home: from left, Scott, Mary Kay, Sue, Joe, David, Diana and Jay. The Paternos have lived in the same house since 1969.**

taught his kids to play poker, and they gambled with chips. Hearts, pinochle . . . you name it, the Paternos played it. Now when the family gathers, everyone plays Trivial Pursuit — boys vs. girls. The boys get all of the orange sports questions right. The girls do well on the other categories, including the brown literature ones.

"But unfortunately, they have Joe," Sue says. "He's good, too."

Fortunately for Joe, he has Sue on his team in all but Trivial Pursuit. In the foreword to "Paterno: By the Book," Random House senior vice president and editor Sam Vaughan referred to Sue as Joe's "not-so-secret weapon."

"She does more in one day," says Nittany Lion Club executive director Kay Kustanbauter, "than most of us do in six months."

Sue spends much of August canning spaghetti sauce and other such items and making roasted peppers that she can freeze. "It's really tiring," says Mary Kay, the Paternos' second-oldest. "Sometimes you say, 'Why don't you get someone to do this?' "

But for Sue, that's not an option. "And it's not paper plates and napkins," Kustanbauter says. "It's china, linen, crystal. But they make it so homey."

Kustanbauter's favorite is Sue's gingerbread cookies. Joe has raved about his wife's spaghetti sauce on his weekly call-in radio show. And everyone knows all about Sue's roasted peppers.

One of her featured entrees is timbale, an elaborate dish that Sue makes entirely from scratch. She makes her own crepes. Her own sauce. Cuts up chicken and meatballs into tiny pieces. Layers the whole thing in a pan. It's a ton of work — just ask Mary Kay, who helped her mom make it once.

"She offered to give me the recipe," Mary Kay says. "I was like, don't bother. But if you have any leftovers, I'll take them."

At one fund-raising event, a donor paid $5,000 just to have dinner with Joe and Sue — not just for bragging rights among his fellow alumni, but because he knew it would be a pleasant evening.

"They're alike in what they believe," Kustanbauter says.

The Paternos are No. 1 with Penn State fans during a national championship parade through State College after the 1987 Fiesta Bowl.

"But as far as personalities, Sue is more the character."

Joe always calls himself "not a phone guy;" Sue is the first person on the phone to a friend to offer congratulations or condolences. Joe is serious, usually excusing himself from post-game festivities at his house to go upstairs and watch film; Sue is silly, once pouring water-based orange paint over the Nittany Lion shrine to get the campus fired up for the Syracuse game.

They are alike, too, in their devotion to their new grandchildren. Sue needs "a fix" about every three weeks. Both she and Joe read to Brian, Matthew and Olivia when they come to visit, and Joe — much to the surprise of his daughters — has become a hands-on grandpa. He'll get on the floor with them, give them horsey-back rides through the house.

And after one party, Joe came downstairs and offered to sit with Olivia while everyone else cleaned up. He and his granddaughter sat in a chair and talked to each other, and after five minutes, they were curled up together, asleep.

Says Kustanbauter, "You know how some people call their grandpa 'Pop-Pop.' Someone said we should call Joe 'Joe-Pa-Pop.' "

Joe and Sue have tried to use their position in the community to do good. They have donated thousands of dollars to Penn State, and their devotion to raising money for a better library will result in the addition to Pattee Library — where they first met — being called the Paterno Library.

They work with the Special Olympics, the College of Liberal Arts, the United Way. Sue offers communion to students who attend Mass on Saturday afternoons at the Penn State Catholic Center. "She's the most hands-on honorary chair I've ever been around," Kustanbauter says.

And they have made the Paterno name practically synonymous with Penn State.

Says Kustanbauter, "Just as Joe and Sue have been a good marriage, Penn State and Joe have been that good of a marriage."

JOE & SUE PATERNO
1

CLOSE, BUT NO CIGARS

CHAPTER FOUR

BY GENE COLLIER

"S MOTT" IS THE WORD Joe Paterno has always used for evidence of applied intelligence.

"He's an awfully good football playuh," the coach has said hundreds upon hundreds of times about hundreds upon hundreds of awfully good football players. "He's big; he's tough; he's smott."

The Brooklyn-raised son of Italian immigrants, the coach himself is real smott, having not only been to Brown to study literature, but having cultivated over most of a century an appreciation of language and art and culture so genuine that he knows stuff well beyond where the semicolons go in sample quotations.

But as the 1970's advanced on Penn State, Paterno, smott as he was, probably was not prepared for the byproducts of the great social convulsion that was the 60's. Suddenly, the sometimes maddeningly idyllic campus was no longer populated strictly by young men and women whose focus was framed principally by scholarship and dental hygiene.

Vietnam was raging.

In a flash of rifle fire at Kent State, an era of student anguish and outrage over the war and the role of government in an expanding society came to the self-fulfilling prophecy of then California Governor Ronald Reagan, whose position on quelling widespread protests was, "If it takes a bloodbath, then let's get it over with."

The bloody race riots that had exploded all over urban America through the 60's were still spreading toxic rhetoric and emotion to previously unaffected outposts as the 70's began.

"I thought we might have — it turned out we didn't but I thought we might have — a problem after a *Sports Illustrated* article about our black kids in the late 60's," Paterno recalls. "We had a lot of problems on this campus. Students took over Old Main. I was out of town one time when Mike Reid

and some other guys wanted to go up there and pull people out and things like that. George Welsh was on the staff at the time and George and his neighbor, a geology teacher, really talked Reid and those guys into staying out of it.

"I remember when I got back, we had Charlie Pittman on that team, and we sat down and talked. I was really unaware about how people felt about some things. But Charlie said, 'No, I really don't think you have that problem here, coach.'

"But it definitely, definitely forced me into having a dialogue. To this day, any time there's something like that, I'm very comfortable sitting down and talking about it. We had a problem one time where, for some reason or another, I wanted to get Lydell and Franco and some others out to the house. They came out in a couple of cars and eight or nine big black kids came into the house. I remember Lydell sayin', 'There goes the neighborhood, coach.' "

In April of 1970, two months after a special committee appointed by Penn State President Eric A. Walker recommended that "the university must recognize it is not dealing with a host of irrational black students' protests aimed at getting 'whitey,' " relations between administrators and the campus' seething cadres of anti-war protesters and black demonstrators climaxed in an ugly confrontation with the state police.

Eighteen State Troopers were injured with rocks, fires were set in nine dormitories, windows were broken and Walker's home was vandalized, forcing him and his wife to flee in the middle of the night.

This was the dizzying political climate in which the winningest decade of Paterno's career began, and it was the most trying, most bittersweet decade as well.

"A lot of us participated in those demonstrations after the Cambodian invasion and we all felt very strongly about it," said Doug Allen, a Penn State linebacker of that era and now the assistant executive director of the National Football League Players Association. "Universities all over the country were in turmoil. One of the good things to come out of it was that it bonded us and the team managed to thrive in that environment.

"One of the nice things about Penn State was that you could think for yourself. You were not locked up in an athletic dorm and told to mind your own business. You were permitted some intellectual freedom."

Paterno feels even today that he was just young enough (43 at the time) and just smott enough to let freedom ring for those children of the 60's.

"I thought that it was good that those things happened to me when I was young, when I was a young coach," Paterno says. "If none of that had happened and all of a sudden you're 65 years old and a bunch of kids are doing some things that you don't like, I don't know how I would have reacted.

"I might have gotten on my high horse. Been autocratic."

Might, in fact, have alienated the core group of kids who would make Penn State's next gallant run at a national championship in 1973, many of whom were on campus in the fall of 1969 and were redshirted along the way. The 1969 freshman team fashioned a unique Penn State kinship. They practiced against Reid, Steve Smear, Dennis Onkotz.

When the great Lion teams led by those players went unbeaten in 1968 and 1969 and did not finish atop the polls, that freshman team assumed the mission with no way of knowing it would be tortured with the same fate.

Penn State lost three of the first five games the year after Reid & Co. left town. Got scalded by four touchdowns at Colorado in September of 1970, and losses at Tennessee in 1971 and 1972 kept Paterno's team from any legitimate claim to something other than grudging national status as a very good program for which notarized greatness was still out of the question.

Skunked 14-0 by Oklahoma in the Sugar Bowl following the 1972 season, Paterno's seventh Penn State team finished 10th in the final Associated Press poll, a slot that looked not only appropriate but almost comfortable. Penn State had some awfully good football players, but Penn State was not

Paterno leads by example during spring practice, driving his shoulder into a sled to demonstrate blocking technique. Right, the Coach kicks back.

Oklahoma, not Nebraska, not Notre Dame, not Alabama, not Ohio State. It was on a cluttered second shelf of college football's interchangeables.

But the next official protest of that notion — the next figurative occupation of the administration building — was about to begin, and without anyone really feeling it.

"If they didn't give the title to the (unbeaten) '68 and '69 teams," said Allen, "it was hard to understand how we could ever get it."

There were a variety of other mixed signals.

Paterno went to bed one night in the summer of 1973 having agreed to become the head coach and part owner of the New England Patriots, but awoke in the middle of the night with the decision that it didn't "feel right."

The quarterback question for the fall of 1973 wasn't answered until August, when Paterno decided inexperienced junior Tom Shuman would do as the rather nondescript successor to the amazingly resourceful John Hufnagel.

"A typical Penn State quarterback," recalls Johnny Majors, then the Pitt coach. "Slow-footed, not very quick, not too colorful, but he got the job done."

Fortunately for Shuman, there was someone standing five yards behind him who was as quick and colorful as anything Penn State would need in the fall of 1973, a converted defen-

90

sive back from Upper Darby who'd walk into an engine room vacated by Lydell Mitchell and Franco Harris and actually increase the output.

John Cappelletti did that with strength and speed of course, but he further brought to the position a unique sense and style that has never been described any better than it was in the student newspaper that fall. "Cappelletti," the writer said, moves like "a man bicycling in heavy traffic."

"I blocked for Franco and Lydell my sophomore year," Mark Markovich remembers. "Nothing has to be said about their stature, but we did not miss a beat when Cappy took over as a junior. He didn't look at first glance like he was a knifing-type runner, but he was.

"It was very easy to block for him. Cappy had the ability to find a crease and get there. I did a lot of pulling and when I was pulling for a sweep, I didn't have to worry about anything but running in the path I was supposed to run in. Cappy would set up defenders so that they had to go through me to get to him. He didn't have the greatest speed, but his style made up for that, and yet when he exploded, he would take off and nobody would catch him."

When Penn State left to start the season at Stanford on Sept. 13, there was little doubt that Cappelletti was primarily responsible for what it wanted to accomplish, but few people on that plane to California knew how dominant an offensive player he'd become over the next three months.

Penn State maneuvered past Stanford, 20-6, then outscored its next six opponents, 292-62, as Cappelletti, well, found some creases and got there.

"That was a great team," Paterno said. "Any team that had Cappelletti had a chance to beat you."

That particular autumn was warm and gorgeous in Central Pennsylvania, and Beaver Stadium crowds that averaged a then-capacity 59,000 routinely streamed away when Paterno put No. 22 back in the barn early in the second half. But on Nov. 10, with the temperature dipping into the low 30's and a biting wind sliding down Mount Nittany all afternoon, North Carolina State solved Penn State's elegant defensive schemes for 29 points, more than three times the average yield to that point. In their seats long past what was comfortable on a

howling, gray afternoon, 59,424 stayed for all of what was likely Cappelletti's greatest performance.

Cappelletti carried an incredible 41 times for 220 yards against the desperate Wolfpack, dragging Penn State to a 35-29 season-saving victory. It was his third consecutive 200-yard game. No one in NCAA history had ever done that.

For his 1,522 yards and 17 touchdowns for an unbeaten team, Cappelletti was awarded the Heisman Trophy, emblematic of at least some sort of establishment "best." But when the Lions finished the season with easy victories over Ohio University and Pitt and wound up 12-0, the idea that this particular team was as special as any in the school's history began to float.

"I think we had both the talent and the spirit to beat anybody," Markovich says. "There was a feeling that no matter

who we would have played against, somehow, somebody would have found a way to do the job. Chuck Herd would have made a one-handed catch or Eddie O'Neil would have come up with a interception or Randy Crowder with a sack.

"We were such a community for the entire period. We were in different fraternities or maybe different dorms, but we did not go our separate ways. I think in spite of the All-Americans we had, we were still basically overachievers."

Crowder, the carnivorous defensive tackle from Farrell, and O'Neil, the textbook inside linebacker out of Warren, joined Cappelletti on the All-America team, but Markovich's assessment is historically correct.

"That team was not as physically dominant as some teams we've had here," Paterno said. "But the '73 squad was a very close bunch of kids. Ed O'Neil, Mark Markovich, those were solid, solid kids. They'd go out and they'd *play ya!* You might beat 'em, but you'd have to be damn good to beat 'em. You'd better not make any mistakes because they aren't going to make any. That was a smott football team."

That smottness, if you will, was only a direct reflection of the head coach.

"We never panicked, I know that," Allen says. "We liked to see teams that would come out and jump up and down and start doing a lot of yelling. Our thing was to start out playing well and then build the tempo so that we were playing our best football in the second half, and that was the way Joe wanted it. He didn't waste a lot of time and energy on locker room histrionics, with the exception of when he got angry with us. He tried to say in as few words as possible what needed to be said. He let the emotional team leaders do the screaming.

"Once the players kicked the coaches out at halftime of the Pitt game and Tom Donchez was yelling about something, and he threw his helmet on the locker room floor and it bounced up and knocked Greg Buttle cold. But Joe's message

[**Paterno has always been popular with Penn State fans, always taking time out to sign autographs for a group of admirers.**]

93

was only that if we've done everything right and we stay intense and focused and we're a better team, we'll win. That was kind of inherent in the program. You don't panic. You just keep getting better throughout the game."

How good Penn State was as it prepared to meet LSU in the 1974 Orange Bowl was again not an issue weighing on the national consciousness, but Paterno went to Miami feeling like the ever more maddeningly elusive national championship was not entirely out of reach given the right chain reaction of bowl results.

"I don't know if we had as big a right to the national title then as we did some other times, even though we were 12-0," Paterno said. "That was the year Notre Dame beat Alabama in a great game" in the Sugar Bowl. "I was watching it in my suite in Miami and I thought we had a chance until Notre Dame won that game."

The next night, LSU held Penn State to nine first downs and Cappelletti to a season-low 50 yards on 26 carries, but still didn't keep these Lions from a spectacularly uncolorful 16-9 victory. Herd caught a 72-yard touchdown pass from Shuman in the second quarter, and Cappelletti managed a one-yard touchdown run on an achy ankle as Penn State won for the 12th straight time and the 33rd time in the last 36 games played by Paterno's seniors.

The polls that came out in the morning placed them fifth.

"Looking back at it I can honestly say I had zero disappointment," Markovich says. "The fact that the sports writers and coaches did not deem us worthy at the time; that didn't affect us then and it doesn't affect me now. It was just such a glamorous season with Cappy winning the Heisman that the fact that the media and coaches didn't vote us No. 1, I thought was really insignificant. At the end of that season when we won the Orange Bowl, Paterno came into the locker room, stood there and gave us a very quick talk, and his presentation was this: 'There's only one poll that matters and that's our poll. In our poll, we're No. 1.' There was nothing but joy and glee in that locker room."

Paterno emerged from that scene and pronounced the 1973 Lions "the best team I've ever had," but Allen doesn't believe it to this day.

Paterno takes his role as educator as seriously as his job as coach. Above, an honorary doctorate from Gettysburg College in 1979. Below, he gives PSU's 1973 commencement speech.

"The hell he did," Allen says. "He thought his 1969 team was."

And that's probably correct.

"The '73 team didn't play a lot of tough teams," Paterno says now. "They didn't have to go to Alabama or play Nebraska, that sort of thing. But they were fighters. A lot of good kids. But even the LSU team we beat in the Orange Bowl was not a great team. They played well that night, but they had three losses. It was not like beating Missouri or Kansas," ranked seventh and sixth respectively in consecutive Orange Bowls, as the '68 and '69 teams had done.

"That was back in the days when the schedule didn't get the respect it deserved," says Allen. "We'd played four bowl teams and some of the teams that finished ranked ahead of us had been beaten. We didn't feel like we were getting enough respect for who we played and that was the reason that Joe started scheduling Alabama, Notre Dame and Nebraska."

By the time those confrontations came around, Paterno had built a couple of teams that surpassed in pure athletic giftedness and multi-dimensional firepower the 1973 model, but superb gamesmanship and savvy have not been seen since.

Welsh, the Virginia coach Paterno credits with helping avoid a potentially program-rattling incident at the launch of the 70's, was in Beaver Stadium as head coach at Navy on Sept. 21, 1974, and coaxed the Midshipmen to an incredible 7-6 upset that, combined with a 12-7 Lou Holtz victory over Paterno at North Carolina State that November, ultimately left State at No. 7 in the final polls.

Paterno's '75 and '76 teams would lose eight times, including a thorough second-half spanking in a 24-7 loss to eventual national champion Pitt. When Notre Dame slapped the Lions, 20-9, in the 1976 Gator Bowl, Penn State finished a season unranked for the first time since 1966, Paterno's first year as head coach.

But by early 1977, he already had the pieces in place for Penn State's best run ever at a national title.

After all, he was smott.

ALMOST . . .

THE HEARTBREAK OF 1978

HE WAS ALL BUT FINISHED with his 29th season at Penn State and his 13th as head coach when Joe Paterno finally elevated this decorated program into a position where he could dock it with a national championship merely by winning a football game.

It had never been quite that simple, but in the last week of December 1978, Penn State was the No. 1 team in America, and in the too-few instances when the No. 1 team beats the No. 2 team on New Year's Day, it need not fear any amount of convoluted polling and it need not fear any spastic presidential decree.

All that could deny Penn State its first national title after 92 years was Alabama, for which the undefeated Lions harbored no undue fear either.

"We had the better team," Paterno says today.

But near college football's summit, the air was thin.

The delicious freedom and recklessness of New Orleans intensified in the streets as the Sugar Bowl approached, and Pete Fountain was planning his New Year's Eve party at the Hilton (only $50), but Paterno was feeling none of that energy or anticipation. He was claustrophobic.

"I saw (Florida coach) Steve Spurrier at the Hall of Fame dinner in New York the week before he left to play in a national championship game for the first time against Nebraska," Paterno said. "He said, 'Can you give me any advice?' And I said, 'Yeah, Steve; no matter what you think, it's gonna be *worse*. It's like you went to the Super Bowl.' I said, 'It's *unbelievable*.' "

The national attention aimed at a No. 1 vs. No. 2 Sugar Bowl between Joe Paterno and Bear Bryant was as hot as it got in that era, and immense packs of media were everywhere from the French Quarter to Penn State's practice facility at ratty Tulane Stadium to the lobby of the Hilton.

"I couldn't get out of the hotel," Paterno said. "I couldn't

do anything. I couldn't even go to church."

In his suite, Paterno fretted and stared at the television. Three nights before the biggest football game of his life, he watched Woody Hayes punch Clemson linebacker Charlie Bauman in the final minute of the Gator Bowl, ending the Ohio State icon's great and (until then) noble coaching career. In less than 72 hours, Paterno would feel like ending his own.

It had taken the Penn State coach four seasons after the unbeaten autumn of 1973 to collect and develop the right combination of muscle and will necessary to make yet another run at the maddeningly unattainable national title.

Most of the elements had been in place now for two years. In fact, the seniors Paterno took with him to New Orleans had lost only one of their previous 23 games, a 24-20 decision at Kentucky in October of 1977. The launch coordinates for the spotless season climaxing at this Sugar Bowl were Tempe, Ariz., and Christmas Day of the previous year.

It was there and then that Chuck Fusina and Matt Suhey and Bob Torrey and a frighteningly destructive defense led by sophomore defensive tackles Matt Millen and Bruce Clark scorched Arizona State in its own stadium in the Fiesta Bowl, 42-30.

That game wasn't over for 10 minutes before Millen and Clark, the emotional axis of Paterno's club, started talking about 1978 and the sacrifice and commitment it would take to win everything. Everything.

It would take another All-America season from offensive tackle Keith Dorney, the massive technician from Allentown who'd go on to play nine seasons with the Detroit Lions.

It would take an All-America season from place-kicker Matt Bahr, who'd play 17 NFL seasons.

It would take an All-America season from Fusina, the quarterback from McKees Rocks who'd win the Maxwell Award as the nation's outstanding player.

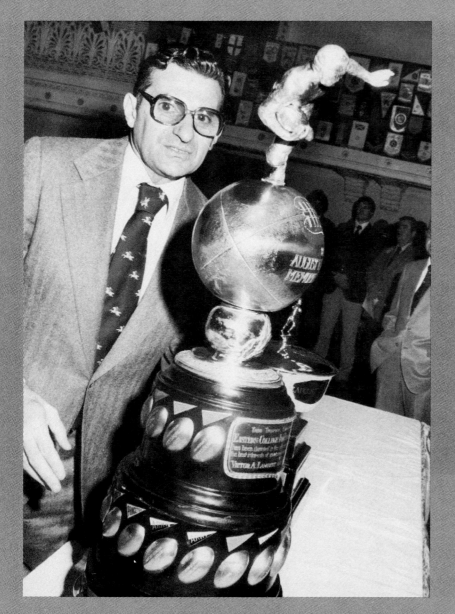

[Nov. 30, 1978, New York City: Joe Paterno accepts the Lambert Trophy for the 10th time in his 13 years as head coach.]

"I always felt that that team, of all the teams I've been around, had the best sense of exactly what everybody was supposed to be doing," says Tom Bradley, a defensive back in 1978 and one of Paterno's defensive assistants since 1979. "Everybody had a role on that team. Everybody knew their particular place and fit together extremely well. Everybody knew who was throwing the ball, who was catching it; there wasn't a lot of internal conflict."

But for all of its thick ability, laser focus, and singularity of purpose, it nearly derailed on the preposterous karma that somehow attached itself to the otherwise mindless task of playing Temple in Philadelphia.

On Sept. 6, 1975, at Franklin Field, some of these same Lions escaped the West Philly night with a 26-25 victory over the lightly regarded Owls. On October 30, 1976, the nucleus of this Penn State powerhouse got out of Veterans Stadium with a second consecutive one-point win over Temple, 31-30. And still no one connected to the 1978 team felt any sense of danger when it kicked off the season and the Labor Day weekend Friday night, Sept. 1, 1978 at Veterans Stadium.

It would take an All-America season from Pete Harris, the instinctive safety with the kind of big play aptitude once demonstrated at Penn State by his older brother, Franco.

Most especially, it would take the kind of defiant excellence most consistently demonstrated by the inseparable Millen and Clark, roommates, soulmates, partners in grime, who would put together All-America performances barely six feet from each other on Paterno's defensive line and remain as prominent defensive players in the NFL throughout the next decade.

Bahr nailed the first of his 22 field goals that night.

It was a good thing he did. It came in the game's final minutes and it snapped a nearly unthinkable and otherwise entirely forgettable 7-7 tie.

"There was a lot of apprehension when we lined up for that field goal," center Chuck Correal remembers. "You're thinking, all this talent, all these weapons, the table was kind of set for us to make some noise nationally and maybe grab the brass ring. We were nervous. But we had confidence in Matt."

The wooosh of relief with Bahr's kick and the 10-7 final was felt all the way back to State College, but it did little to reinforce the assumption that Penn State was strong enough to have its way with Ohio State in Columbus in two weeks.

Paterno's team crept into Ohio 2-0. Victories over Temple and Rutgers by a combined 19 points weren't the kind of thing that would make Woody Hayes cower in the film room. Hayes thought just enough of Penn State that he elected to start a freshman quarterback against the Lion defense. Art Schlichter got to start his Ohio State career on the same day that Paterno's celebrated defense finally bared its teeth.

Schlichter was intercepted five times when he wasn't having his skeleton rattled. Penn State 19, Ohio State 0.

In Paterno's career as a head coach, Penn State had run itself up against the Ohio State dynasty only twice, losing 17-9 in 1975 and 12-7 in 1976. The 1978 clearing of that ominous scarlet and gray hurdle finally ignited these Lions.

Over the next five games, Penn State outscored its opponents 208-57, setting up a Nov. 4 collision with fifth-ranked Maryland in Beaver Stadium. Maryland was trying everything to become a primary player in the kind of competitive Eastern football that Paterno relentlessly promoted. Its weight program had produced a roster Paterno thought might even be stronger than his own, and he opened the game with a fancy misdirection screen pass that signaled an emphasis on State's still-superior athleticism.

Before leaving his house that Friday to stay overnight with the team, Paterno told his wife, Sue, that he had a very good feeling about this game.

Penn State 27, fifth-ranked Maryland 3. Fusina turned up on the cover of *Sports Illustrated* under the seemingly urgent headline PENN STATE ROLLS ON.

"We had several really big showdowns, but even those games, we felt we should win," says Correal, now a Pittsburgh investment broker. "That team really did have a lot of confidence. I don't think the type of guy Joe recruits for Penn State would ever be openly brazen about it. It took the form of just going out there expecting to win. That's been the history of Penn State since Joe's been there."

After putting together conservative, back-to-back, bad-

weather victories at home against North Carolina State (19-10) and Pitt (17-10), Penn State accepted a bid to meet 10-1 Alabama in the Superdome. The Lions had a 19-game winning streak in progress and every last earmark of destiny in their bearing.

On the morning of Jan. 1, 1979, the Crescent City awoke with its regularly scheduled brain-tumor hangover and the Nittany Lions filed into the magnificent auditorium off Poydras Street, climbed into their classic all-white night nurse uniforms and put on, for the first time in their history, white shoes.

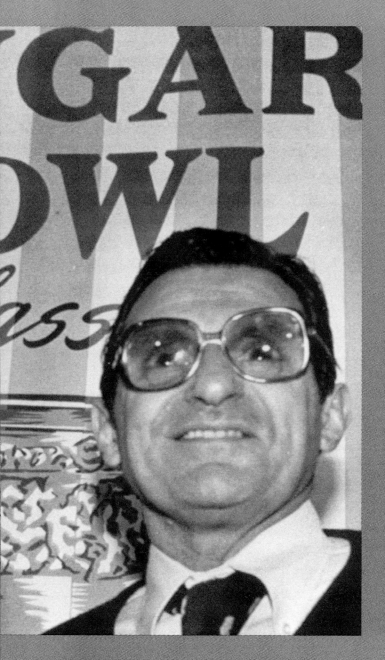

place opposite the legendary Bear, whom he revered, and who he noticed was not wearing the trademark houndstooth hat, as a Southern gentleman always removes his hat indoors, especially when ladies are present.

Paterno perhaps also noted, for the final time, that the weeks of preparation he'd just completed did not end the way he wanted them to.

"That experience changed my philosophy on bowl games," he said. "My theory on getting ready for bowl games had always been to keep some things back to give them at the bowl site. I found that if you give them everything and they're ready when they get to the bowl site, they get in trouble. Hopefully they'll have a lot of pride and you can appeal to it.

"You can say, 'You guys are so lousy in practice and this is such a big game and TV and all of that, let's get going.' And some kid will say, 'OK, let's get to work, let's enforce the curfew, all of that.' But I went down to that game with the same approach and I didn't get a darn thing done."

Whatever he'd planned to get done to guarantee protection for Fusina certainly was not in evidence. Alabama showed some blitzes it hadn't all season, and the spectacle of the Lion quarterback under early and ferocious pressure was the first clear indication that this day would be all uphill.

"I remember Chuck Fusina coming off the field early in the game," says Johnny Majors, the former Pitt coach who was scouting that game after his first year at Tennessee, "and when he got to the hash mark he held his hands out to Joe like, 'What can I do?' and I remember thinking, 'Uh-oh; they're frustrated.' I was fond of Fusina. I'd tried to recruit him in high school. I felt bad for the young man."

Fusina was on his way to seven sacks and a Penn State bowl record of four interceptions, and the fact that he somehow kept this Sugar Bowl a 60-minute affair was a small monument to him on a horrible afternoon.

"I think we were probably trying to do too many things," Bradley says. "The first offensive play we had went for about nine yards out to the 29, but the backside tackle was called for holding and all of a sudden we're back at the 10. We never got out of that hole the whole first half."

The figurative hole Alabama was in seemed just as deep,

[The Sugar Bowl pitted two of college football's
greatest coaches against one another: Alabama's
Paul (Bear) Bryant against Paterno.]

"White shoes were really in vogue then," Correal says. "A lot of guys had always wanted to wear them instead of the black ones we always wore, and that was the first game Joe ever let us do it. We wore Adidas basketball shoes because somebody had determined that they were the best for that kind of (artificial) turf. They were low, white shoes with three black stripes on them."

Paterno sprinted to the Penn State sideline and took his

but at just about the moment when the 76,824 people inside the Superdome figured they'd seen a scoreless first half, Alabama quarterback Jeff Rutledge fired a 30-yard pass into the end zone to Bruce Bolton, who made a diving catch with eight seconds on the clock.

"Pete Harris says to this day that that pass hit the carpet," Correal says. "There were so many what-ifs in that game."

In the third quarter, Penn State painstakingly began to pull the momentum back. Harris seemed to accomplish it when he picked off a Rutledge pass at the 'Bama 48. Fusina hit Mike Guman for 25 yards on a third down play to the 19 and after Guman ran for two yards, Fusina nailed Scott Fitzkee in the back of the end zone with a game-tying touchdown.

But on a day when there were no less than 20 punts, not all of them were going into history in total obscurity. Total obscurity was the location at which little-used running back Lou Ikner stood in everyone's consciousness when he accepted a Penn State punt at his own 27 and blasted 62 yards down

[**Scott Fitzkee scored Penn State's only touchdown with this end-zone catch.**]

the carpet to the Penn State 11. On third down from the 8, Major Ogilvie pounded his way into the Lion end zone to re-erect Alabama's seven-point lead.

It was 14-7.

And it is 14-7.

And 14-7 it always will be.

But the story of this great game's final seven minutes, the story of how it almost wasn't 14-7, remains perhaps the most compelling chapter of Penn State lore regardless of national championships no one could be sure were coming in the decade to follow.

As the Superdome clock flashed past 7:00, Lion defensive end Joe Lally recovered an Alabama fumble 19 yards from the Tide goal line. Suhey gained 11 yards to the eight, and then, on second-and-goal from the 8, Fusina found Fitzkee again on a crossing route that moved the ball to the 1. Fitzkee's catch at that spot was as critical as anything that followed, because for a tenth of a second that seemed like a century, Fitzkee appeared to run parallel to the goal line as he tried to avoid All Southeast Conference cornerback Don McNeal, who was on approach from the opposite direction.

"That's the one play I remember most," Bradley says. "I was standing on the sideline at about the 40, but I remember thinking that if Scott had just fallen down there he'd have been in the end zone. McNeal had come off his man so quickly in the end zone. What made him turn and come flying out there? It was one of those things that made me feel like we'd never win."

On third-and-goal from the 1, State sent Suhey straight over Correal.

"I remember being on the ground and looking up in the air and seeing Matt Suhey above me; I thought he scored," Correal says. "My body was kind of straddling the goal line and from that vantage point, I thought his momentum took him past me, but he was knocked back closer to where my body started."

Officials marked the ball six inches from the goal line.

In the next few seconds, Paterno made a decision that would haunt him so severely that he nearly took himself out of the profession.

"You think I didn't second-guess myself? I was mad at myself and mad at my coaching staff. They talked me out of it. I didn't want to run it again. I wanted to throw the ball. I let them talk me out of it. That's not their fault. It's my fault. I'm supposed to make those decisions.

"I lost my guts."

Barry Krauss did not lose his. The splendid Tide linebacker who would spend 13 seasons in the NFL with the Colts and Dolphins had helped stop Suhey on third down, and he was pretty sure the same thing was coming on fourth down.

The handoff was to Guman this time, but the point of attack hadn't been altered. Krauss launched himself toward Guman at the goal line, met him head to head six inches on the other side of it, and both fell to the carpet on opposite sides of a mountain of muscle, an image preserved in oil that hangs in Alabama's athletic dorm to this day.

Krauss busted his helmet and almost knocked himself out.

"Putting time between us now and 1978 has taken a lot of the edge off it," Correal says. "In the first months and years after it I felt more defensive about it. It was such a memorable play. Alabama had everybody bunched in there. They had two men in the gaps between me and the guards and they had another guy head up on me and then two linebackers. It was really five on three. I had had a good game that day. I was trying to get to Barry Krauss. I couldn't get there. There was too much traffic. I knocked back the guy I was into and if they'd been in some kind of normal defense I would have gotten there."

If those unforgettable minutes were not cruel enough for

Alabama's Jim Bob Harris (9) steals a pass intended for Penn State receiver Bob Bassett.

[**Alabama stops Lions halfback Mike Guman in a memorable fourth-quarter, goal-line stand.**]

Penn State, the what-ifs did not end there. The enduring freeze-frame of that fourth-and-inches pileup is indelible in college football history, but it didn't end the game.

"People don't realize it," Paterno says, "but when they stopped us, we still had a couple of minutes to play in the game."

Oh yes they do.

"We made them kick the ball out of the end zone. The kid shanks the ball and puts it on the 20-some yard line. We're out of timeouts but we still have some time."

And now, the final what-if flourish.

What if Penn State hadn't had 12 players on the field for the punt?

What if the Penn State sideline hadn't called attention to that fact by screaming at the punt receiving team to shed one player?

Finally, what if Paterno had had someone more responsible than a graduate assistant making substitutions?

"We had 12 kids on the field," Paterno says, completing the memory. "So they get a 15-yard first down and we can't stop the clock. And I had a G.A. making substitutions."

Still, that part of it doesn't bother the head coach like the play call of fourth and one.

"I said stuff after the game like, 'If we can't make that much we don't deserve to win the national championship.' Well, that sounds good, but it's a lot of nonsense. That was the most frustrating game I've ever coached. We had it there. We had a better team. I almost gave up coaching that year.

"I went back to New York. Back home to Brooklyn, took the subway out there. Walked around my old parish, my old neighborhood. I was gonna get out of it. I was so p.o.'d at myself because those kids, they only lost two games in two years.

"I thought maybe I'd do something else. Thank God I changed my mind."

Penn State never wore white shoes again.   — G.C.

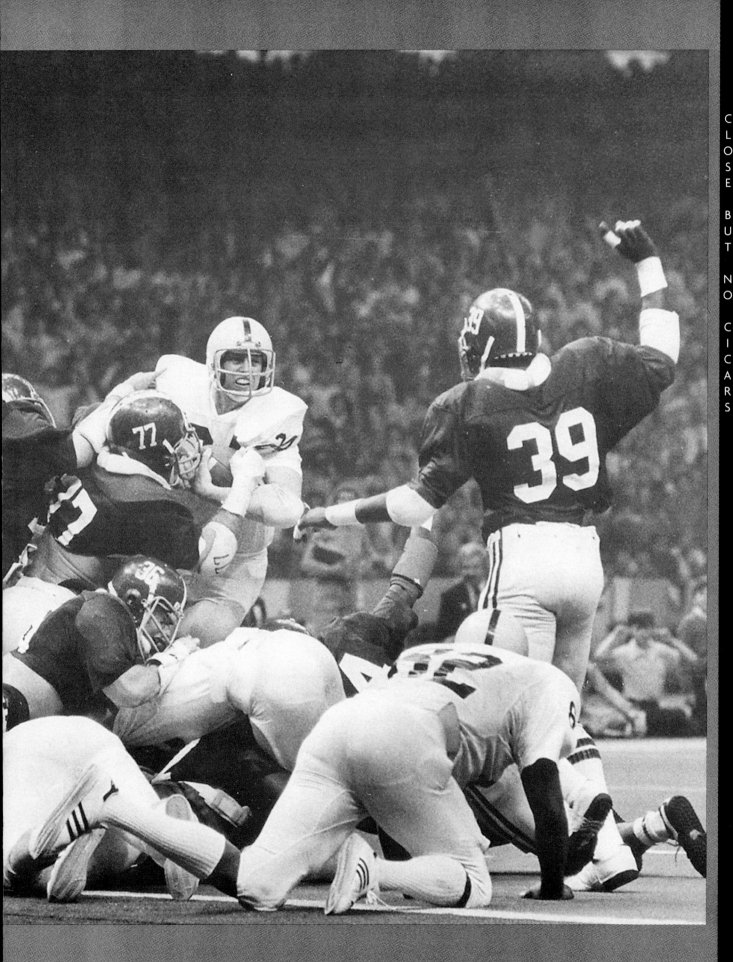

CLOSE BUT NO CIGARS

CHAPTER FIVE

BY CHUCK FINDER

ET IT BE WRITTEN, let it be recorded, that Joe Paterno's national-championship jaunt through the 1980's all began nine days before the decade.

Go back to 1979. Penn State frittered away its best title chance to that point in the Sugar Bowl on New Year's Day 1979. What followed was perhaps Paterno's most distressing campaign to date. The Year After started with the coach stripping the captaincy from star Matt Millen. Two players, including a starting offensive lineman, were suspended after being cited for on-campus drinking. A starting halfback was arrested for drunk driving. Another player got into a bar fight. Yet another broke into a house during the team's Liberty Bowl trip, which ended with an ugly 9-6 victory on Dec. 22, 1979.

Oh, yeah, and this 8-4 Penn State lost its second-most games since Paterno's inaugural head-coaching season, a baker's-dozen years before.

"It carried over to '79," Paterno recalls of that Sugar Bowl gone sour. He went four downs and out against Alabama, whose memorable goal line stand and 14-7 victory wrested the top ranking from Penn State and the national championship so desperately sought by the bespectacled coach and everything Blue and White. The hangover from that defeat caused him to wander the Brooklyn streets of his childhood, wondering if he should continue coaching. He searched. He seethed.

"I was mad at everybody. I was mad at the coaching staff. I wanted to throw the ball down there, but I listened to them. That's not their fault; that's my fault. I'm supposed to make that decision."

[**Dec. 27, 1982, New Orleans: Paterno leaves the practice field in preparation for the Sugar Bowl against the top-ranked Georgia Bulldogs.**]

Paterno couldn't conceal the anguish that lingered through that '79 fall. His self-doubt, his self-loathing were as starkly apparent as his trademark white socks and rolled-up pant cuffs. None of it was pretty.

"You can't fool kids," the coach says, hindsight being 20-20 even behind those thick glasses. "They just know.

"I had some kids go bad on me in '79. That's the worst thing. You've got to have a closure. When you have a bad kid or two, you've got to settle it. Talk to kids. I didn't give a damn, really.

"I was that sour."

So was The Year After.

Millen, an All-America defensive tackle the season before, refused to run distance drills, and his captaincy was yanked. He later opined that Penn State spent all of '79 trying to cope with its Sugar bitterness. "That game was a joke. We had the better team, even the Alabama players knew that. But we got outcoached at the goal line."

Tackle Bill Dugan and a teammate threw away their beers when approached by a resident assistant, but they nonetheless were banished to the sideline. Then, when halfback Booker Moore was arrested off-campus and received a one-week suspension, Dugan growled, "I guess it must be your status on the team that affects your discipline."

Defensive tackle Bruce Clark was injured and missed the season's end. Millen was hurt and ineffective. The offense missed most of the season, or so it seemed. Young talent existed, it was just being stockpiled to give way to veterans. (As one starter described the Penn State quarterbacks, "Dayle Tate is a zero, Frank Rocco is a five and Todd Blackledge" — the redshirted freshman — "is a 10.") If it wasn't being stockpiled, the young talent was too busy fighting locker-room brush fires.

"We had a lot of disagreements between the players and coaches on how things should have been done and how long we should work on this or that," running back Joel Coles would explain four years later. "It was just a bad year for us."

[**Penn State's Curt Warner eludes Georgia's Terry Hoage during the first quarter. He finished with 117 rushing yards and two touchdowns.**]

On Dec. 22, 1979, the Nittany Lions salvaged an eighth victory in the touchdown-less Liberty Bowl — where the last in the too-long line of arrests was made.

The Coach was determined to change with the calendar, with the times.

Sourness turned to bile. Bile turned to anger. Anger turned to conviction.

He gave a damn about winning a national championship. He was going to climb that mountain again, dadgummit. He and Penn State were going to be the last ones standing there, kings of the hill.

It was a pattern Paterno and Penn State would repeat through those championship 80's.

Climb.

Fall off.

Brush off.

Trudge upward again.

Just as every Paterno recruiting class but 1974 wound up undefeated or playing for the national championship during its four years, every recruiting class through the 80's — starting with that 1979 bunch — endured troubles that caused the aging coach to re-evaluate and recommit.

He taught these Lions of the 80's mountain climbing. Two of the teams reached the summit.

"THE ATTITUDE . . . " Greg Gattuso says. "I can remember when I was getting recruited the winter after that 1979 season, Joe was saying — and I heard him say it again after 1984 — 'I've got to get back to the players. I've got to get back to being a hands-on coach. We're going to get tough again.' They were similar."

Come the fall camp of 1980, Paterno infused his team with something heretofore missing: Bull.

Bull in the Ring, that is.

It is football's version of the machismo hair-pull, a drill sim-

[
Paterno rides triumphantly on the shoulders of the national champion Nittany Lions after a 27-23 victory over Georgia in the Sugar Bowl.
]

ilar to the exercise in perspiring pain called the Oklahoma drill. The Bull in the Ring basically is a drill in which teammates attempt to pummel the phlegm from a designated player inside a circle of players, one at a time. In short, it was Paterno's Pamplona.

"He had Sean Farrell and Mike Munchak going after each other," Gattuso recalls of two giants who later became NFL star linemen. "I was in the back of the line praying, 'Please don't let him think I need to be tougher.' It was a senseless exhibition, but it got attention.

"We did up-downs," the then-defensive tackle adds, referring to the brutal form of free-fall push-ups. "We never did up-downs the rest of my four years. My freshman-year camp was a nightmare compared to the others. We were, like, in the military that camp. But I think he was drawing a line in the sand. It was his way. . . . " Or the wrong way.

The Lions began the decade with a pasting of Colgate, 54-10, and lost only once in their first 10 games — by a 21-7 count to Nebraska at Beaver Stadium. In the end, the Lions lost again at home, but to the Pitt team that finished the season ranked No. 2 and was arguably better than national-champion Georgia. Penn State closed the season with a 31-7 spanking of Ohio State and quarterback Art Schlichter in the Fiesta Bowl. It was a start: The team would lose only two bowl games all decade.

You will find folks who contend the 1981 squad was Penn State's best team of the decade. Gattuso is one of them. So is receiver Gregg Garrity, who considers that bunch the most talented of his Penn State tenure.

"We played everybody that was somebody those days," Gattuso says. "I still think the '81 team was the most complete team. What we lacked was a mature (quarterback) Todd Blackledge. We had first-round picks on the offensive line in Farrell and Munchak, and the center was a second-round pick, Jim Romano. We had the makings of the great offense. And I think the defense was probably better that year."

The schedule was a killer, though. Nebraska, Miami, Alabama and Pitt were all Top 10 teams by season's end, but they made up the Lions' share of the regular-season's final nine weeks. Penn State won at Nebraska (30-24), lost at Miami

In 1983, Paterno was honored at San Francisco's Candlestick Park.

NG OUT THE SECOND BALL

E PATERNO
FOOTBALL COACH OF THE
STATE NITTANY LIONS

against a kid named Jim Kelly whom Paterno recruited to play linebacker (17-14), fell at Alabama with star back Curt Warner still injured (31-16) and, two weeks later, visited then-No. 1 Pitt. It was that week's Game of the Century, and Penn State added to the hype.

On Wednesday of that week, Lions defensive stalwart Chet Parlavecchio criticized Pitt's light platter of previous opponents: "Pitt ought to schedule Thiel. . . . We know what it's like to be in a dogfight. They don't." When Pitt staked itself to a quick, 14-0 lead and marched seemingly toward another score, Panthers coach Jackie Sherrill barked at the opposing defense: "Hey, Parlavecchio, whaddya think of our schedule now?"

He barked too soon. Penn State intercepted Pitt's Dan Marino on that third drive, and tacked up two touchdowns to enter halftime at 14-all. Paterno sauntered into the cramped visitors' locker room in the bowels of Pitt Stadium. He gave them a simple speech.

"We got 'em where we want 'em. We're gonna win. OK, adjustments for the second half. . . . "

His Lions, swelling with confidence, proceeded to pummel Pitt the rest of the way. The score lives in the rivalry's infamy. More than a decade later, the mere mention was a surefire way to enrage all things Pitt: 48-14.

Penn State next put the clamps on USC in the Fiesta Bowl, holding Heisman Trophy winner Marcus Allen to 85 yards on 30 carries — his worst performance of the 2,000-yard season by some 62 yards. Clemson was awarded the 1981 national championship because of its undefeated season, but No. 3 Penn State laid a legitimate claim — with two losses and all. "That was incredible," Paterno would say then of the 10-2 finish, "just incredible with the kind of schedule we had." Nevertheless, jilted the same as in the 60's and 70's, Paterno renewed his call for a college-football playoff system.

The 1982 team had the more favorable schedule — Nebraska and Pitt at home, a visit to a below-normal Alabama squad, and no Miami. But did it have the talent? The wherewithal?

"In the beginning, to be honest, I don't think we really thought about that," Gattuso said. The offensive line was rebuilding without Munchak, Farrell and Romano — among 10 NFL draftees gone from the previous season. "We lost a lot of talented people."

Then Paterno and staff retooled the offense. They transformed Penn State — blasphemy — into a passing team. Paterno told the media that August: "We are going to have to throw the ball more."

Have to?

Paterno?

This, of course, likewise shocked many of the Lions. As Gattuso puts it, "Blackledge hadn't torn up the world the year before." The move also ruffled Curt Warner for a time.

Warner was perhaps the most gifted running back ever to dart through the shadows of Mount Nittany. And there were several before him: Lenny Moore, Charlie Pittman, Franco Harris, Lydell Mitchell and Heisman Trophy winner John Cappelletti, to name-drop a few. But Warner outrushed them all.

Paterno and his staff had never heard of Warner, a running back from the bottom of West Virginia, until the kid's English teacher, Libby McKinney, wrote them a letter. Paterno dispatched a part-time coach, Tim Curley, to minuscule Pineville, W.Va., whereupon the future athletic director watched the back proceed to score five touchdowns. On 13 carries.

Paterno and Sherrill found themselves attending Pineville High basketball games, once cheering madly while Warner sank the winning basket with two seconds left to beat rival Mullens. Paterno eventually won, too. Warner chose Penn State.

By Warner's senior season, he had rushed for 2,300 yards and caused hearts to flutter. The coaching staff looked at him, at Blackledge, at junior receivers Kenny Jackson and Kevin Baugh, at tight end Mike McCloskey plus tackles Bill Contz and Ron Heller and figured, you know, this would make a dandy NFL offense. Which it would later, with many of those very players enjoying long pro careers. But, for 1982, Paterno and his assistants attempted to make it a pro-style offense, if not a pro offense.

Air Paterno threw for touchdowns its opening three possessions of 1982 and went from there. This more-open offense let Penn State outlast Maryland in a score-fest (39-31) and rally for a touchdown pass with four seconds left to beat Nebraska

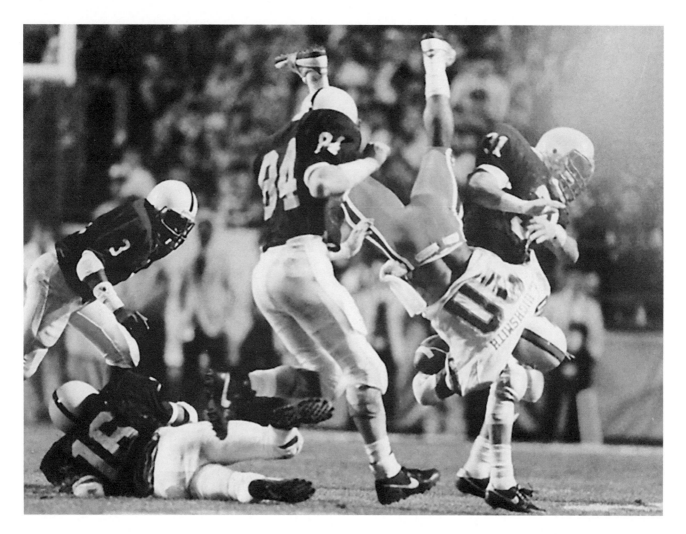

(24-21). Then came three brutal minutes in Alabama.

All it took was that much time to dash hopes of an undefeated season. Protector Mike Suter backed into Ralph Giacomarro's punt, and Alabama got the ball at the Lions' 12. A touchdown and two-point conversion gave the Crimson Tide a 35-21 lead. Just as suddenly, Blackledge threw an interception that was returned for a touchdown. Like that, it was Alabama 42, Penn State 21. "Everyone wrote us off after that," Gattuso recalls. Everyone but Paterno.

"He turned that really big negative into a positive when he walked into our Monday meeting," Gattuso adds. "He told us, 'We did the right thing. You need to lose early if you want to win it all.'

"He was right. We were able to turn it around, and we got good at the end of the year."

The Lions spanked Syracuse, shut out West Virginia and battered Boston College. Victories over North Carolina State

Miami's Alonzo Highsmith goes airborne as he is tackled by Shane Conlan (31) and Keith Karpinski (84) in the third quarter of the 1987 Fiesta Bowl.

and Notre Dame brought Penn State back to Pitt. The result: Another second-half rally by Blackledge, another Lions triumph (19-10). It was the 11th time in his Penn State career that the quarterback brought the Lions back from second-half deficits. Five of those rallies came in fourth quarters.

The 10-1 finish and No. 2 ranking arranged a national-championship date with top-ranked Georgia in the scene of Paterno's grime four years before: the Sugar Bowl. This time, there would be no three unsuccessful plunges into the middle of a Southeastern Conference team's line. There would be no wondering.

After Paterno warned his players at halftime that the game's most important moments would come on the second half's opening possession, Georgia marched 69 yards in 11 plays to pare Penn State's lead to 20-17. Paterno later admitted, "I thought we weren't going to pull it off."

Then Blackledge jump-started the fourth quarter with a 48-yard bomb to a diving Garrity in the end zone — an instant entrant into the pantheon of Highlights in Lions History. Yet it might not have been Garrity's most crucial catch of the day. Soon after Georgia scored to cut the margin to 27-23 with 3:54 left, Blackledge would call on Garrity again. Air Paterno would be on the spot.

Third down and three at the Penn State 32. During the time out, the quarterback told the coach he was going to throw if Georgia aligned in the same defensive formation. *Remember the Paterno lament of the 1979 Sugar? "I wanted to throw the ball down there."*

Blackledge threw a 6-yard pass to Garrity, who offered later, "The outside linebacker missed it by, I'd say, six inches." The completion gave Penn State the first down it needed to run out the clock. It gave Penn State the step it needed to reach the summit.

At long last, Paterno earned his and Penn State's first national championship.

He smiled and said afterward, "I don't think we need a play-off this year."

T HE NEXT SEASON STARTED with three losses — by a collective 100-43.

The season after that ended with a 6-5 record, no bowl for the first time in a decade and a half, and back-to-back losses — by a collective 75-18. The coach called his players "a bunch of babies."

It got worse. In the days after that 1984 debacle, linebacker Carmen Masciantonio, an academic All-America, stated the following for the public prints: "Joe kept trying to fix something that wasn't broken. There was a definite lack of confidence among the players. What he did from there was up to him. To me, it was a disaster."

"It was just a weird year," recalls Gattuso, who was a graduate assistant in 1984 because, well, Paterno told him to come back to State College and finish that degree. "People don't remember it, but that was the year Brigham Young won the national championship. They played Michigan, which was 6-5, too. And Brigham Young wanted Penn State. Joe said we didn't deserve to be in a national-championship game, and he was right;. He just had a belief that it wasn't fair. I had a lot of respect for that type of decision. Even if it did cost me a vacation in San Diego."

The howling renewed, as after the '79 season. The wondering resurfaced. Was Paterno, at 58, too old? Was he over the hill two years after scaling the mountain to No. 1? Was he losing his grip on these players of the so-called Me Decade?

"I can remember getting recruited by Joe," recalls Trey Bauer, a freshman in 1983 and part-time player at linebacker in 1984. "And he said, 'During one of your years, you'll play for the national championship.' After the first two years, I thought, 'I don't think so.'

"But that's the recurring pattern."

Fall off.

Brush off.

Trudge upward again.

"That's why we were successful in '85 and '86," John Shaffer, then the quarterback, says in hindsight. "The disappointment in '84 started that. If we hadn't gone through what we did our sophomore year, I don't think we would have been national champion."

Paterno reined in his schedule, which had grown crammed with banquets, speeches and everything short of department-store openings in the wake of that 1982 national-championship season. He rearranged his staff and, after contemplating retirement again, recommitted himself. He rolled up his sleeves and his pant cuffs. He went back to basics, back to work.

The talent was there, especially on defense. Bauer and fellow linebackers Don Graham and Shane Conlan had been real buggers for Paterno. He used to kick the then-freshmen off the practice field, they were banging up the starters so badly. Bauer's behavior bordered on that of one of those '79 Lions gone astray, and Paterno asked him to transfer after he was thrown out of a study hall.

"I was just a pain in the ass at the time," Bauer recalls. "We had a squad meeting on a Sunday. He came up to me and said, 'Trey, you're never going to play here, so why don't you just transfer? I'll waive your scholarship, I'll get you in anywhere you want to go. But you're never going to play here.'

"I called my father," Bauer said, referring to Charles, his high-school coach in Paramus, N.J. "He said, 'Well, he's right. You're a bum. You have long hair. . . . '

"From there, I had a great career. But you had to buy into Joe's philosophy and his program."

That program faltered a mite in 1983 and 1984, but young Turks such as Bauer, Graham and Conlan joined the coach with the strong convictions in a turning-point offseason before the fall of 1985. "That," Bauer says, "is when it all came to a head."

"In the offseason, Coach Paterno told us about letters people wrote him, telling him he was over the hill," cornerback Duffy Cobbs remembered a year later. "He had a lot to prove to people. It wasn't time for him to leave.

"Joe was *determined*. He instilled that in us from the beginning. He flat out told us, 'We're not going to lose this year.' "

The young Lions didn't lose in 1985.

The old coach hadn't lost his grip.

Now this '85 bunch didn't exactly dazzle. The Lions won their first half-dozen games by a touchdown or less. In the first four of those games, the opposition threw the football into the end zone as time expired, justthatclosetovictory. Each time, Paterno's team prevailed. As if it were willed so. *We're not going to lose.* They didn't until New Year's Day 1986, when they played for the national championship. You'd come a long way, babies.

"I tell you, there was a confidence we had, and it started midway through our junior year," Shaffer says. "That no matter how far we got behind or how things were going, we knew we could win games."

Penn State carried into the Orange Bowl tangible dreams of a second title within four years. Yet two Oklahoma big plays and a loss by No. 2 Miami allowed the Sooners to vault into Penn State's vacated No. 1 spot. Oklahoma gained 132 yards on those two plays, 187 on its other 50. One of the big plays came on an ill-advised blitz call on third-and-24. "I'll never let Jerry (Sandusky, the defensive coordinator) forget it," Paterno says

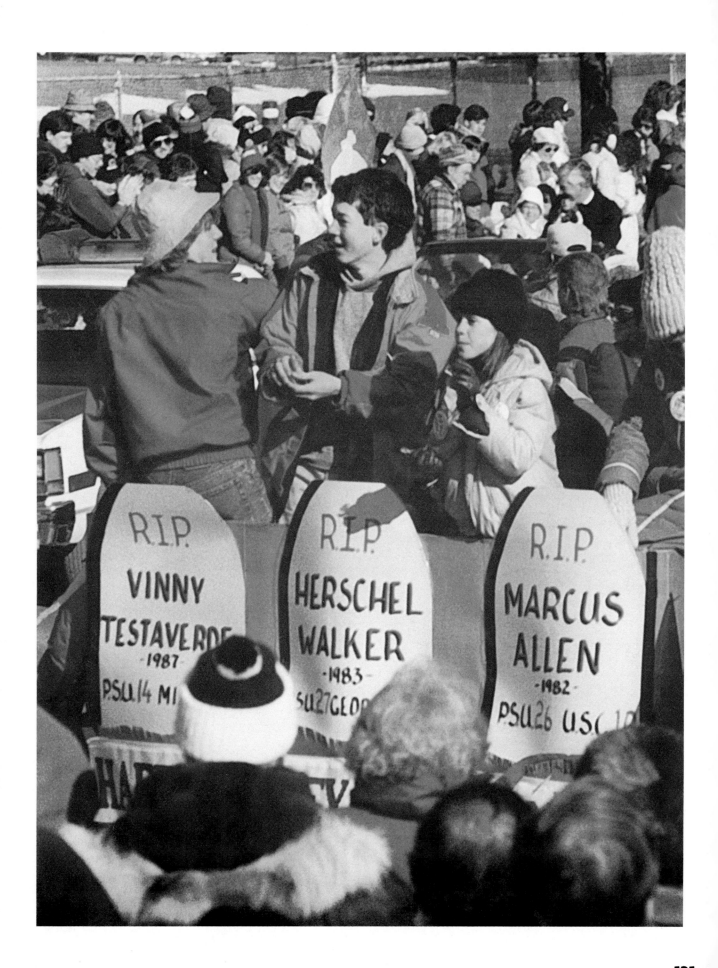

At the White House, Paterno presents a PSU jersey to President Reagan.

with a laugh today. Still, at the time, the Orange left a bitter aftertaste. Another national-championship game. Another Lions loss.

"I'm sorry I had so much to do with the outcome," Shaffer said immediately after the 25-10 defeat. He went 10 for 22 for 74 yards and to the bench with roughly seven minutes left. He had accounted for four of Penn State's five turnovers — three by air, one by land. Paterno agreed that the passing game's failure was a contributing factor, though he told Shaffer not to be so hard on himself.

Paterno also took comfort in this: All along he felt his Lions were a year away.

"I'll never forget the first drive of the game: We took them down the field right away. I'll remember that as long as I live, looking across at [Brian] Bosworth and seeing him huff and puff," Shaffer says. "But that game was very, very disappointing. I was disappointed for the guys who weren't coming back the next year. 'Cause I knew we were talented, that if luck was on our side we'd have another shot."

"We were so much better than those Oklahoma guys, it was scary," Bauer adds. "The next year, there was no way anybody was going to beat us. I think it was even more a sense of urgency. Joe felt he had a special group of guys."

An especially experienced group he had indeed. Sixteen fifth-year seniors. Eighteen returning starters. Thirty-seven of the top 44 back.

Paterno tinkered with the fellows, just the same. He declared the quarterback position an open battle between Shaffer and junior Matt Knizner. (As Shaffer describes it today, "It was going to be a jump ball again.") The coach split them into two offensive units that would see playing time: Shaffer and the Blue boys, Knizner and the Green team. The Harrisburg *Patriot-News* asked readers to vote, and the survey said: Knizner by a 3-to-1 margin.

For Shaffer, it was an even more trying time than the Orange Bowl.

At his grandfather's funeral in March '86, a fellow introduced him as "John Shaffer, the man who lost us the national championship. . . ." Shaffer adds: "Walking into class and having people tell you that you lost the university $75 million

RICHARD NIXON

April 3, 1987

26 FEDERAL PLAZA
NEW YORK CITY

Dear Joe,

Julie told me how much she enjoyed talking to
you at the White House Tuesday night. Since you
were so generous in your references to me, as an
avid football fan, may I return the compliment by
telling you how much I have admired your brilliant
career at Penn State.

Despite the fact that along with the AP, I
named Texas as national champion in 1969, I have
always been a Penn State fan due to the fact that
my uncle, Dr. Ernest Nixon, taught there for over
twenty-five years.

Under separate cover, I am sending you a copy
of my book Leaders for your personal library. I am
also enclosing a copy of the eulogy I gave for one
of your old adversaries on the football field,
Woody Hayes. You and he are very different people
but you have this in common: your players love and
respect you.

With warm regards,

Sincerely,

Richard Nixon

Mr. Joe Paterno

bucks (the estimated value the 1982 title brought the school). That was something people aged 18 to 22 aren't supposed to go through."

Shaffer endured. He threw three touchdowns in the Temple opener, four in the ensuing three games, then took control of the offense — no more Blues or Greens — by the fifth week. Two weeks later, he and the Lions were tip-toeing into Alabama's Bryant-Denny Stadium with a 6-0 record and a No. 6 ranking. Alabama was second-ranked and riding a 13-game unbeaten streak, the nation's longest at the time. The Crimson Tide's defense contained a couple of guys who would go on to rather productive NFL careers: linebackers Derrick Thomas and Cornelius Bennett.

The late Bear Bryant had come to consider the Penn State series a cornerstone to Alabama's national prominence in the 1980's. Paterno, too. "Of all the games we play," the Lions coach said at the time, "this is one we like to play the most. It's two teams with great football traditions, teams that have had great success. When you schedule a game like this, you expect this type of game."

Alabama didn't expect this, though: A whupping. Penn State prevailed by 23-3 as Shaffer — a 40-percent passer on the road heretofore — completed 13 of 17 attempts for 168 yards. D.J. Dozier, rising sophomore Blair Thomas and the rest of Penn State's backs rushed for 210 yards. Even the coach liked what he saw: "Someone has to play awfully well to beat us, the way we're playing," Paterno said.

Maryland (17-15) gave them a fright two weeks later, Notre Dame (24-19) the week after that. It was shades of 1985: Both teams were throwing toward the end zone, trying to conjure the winning points, as time expired. After the dramatic ending at Notre Dame, Shaffer remarked, "There were an awful lot of guys praying on the sideline that never said prayers before."

It wasn't until a season-ending victory over Pitt that the Lions' dream became reality: Penn State vs. Miami, the Fiesta Bowl for the national championship. Heck, NBC loved the idea so much, it pre-empted "Miami Vice" for a day-later game on Jan. 2. This was the first battle between undefeated heavyweights since the Alabama-Notre Dame Sugar Bowl of 1973. This was a Super Bowl-charged atmosphere.

Left, a letter to Paterno from President Nixon, alluding to a slight 18 years earlier. Above, Paterno leads the cheers in Happy Valley.

The Duel in the Desert heated up about the time Miami stepped off its plane in Arizona. Many of the stars donned army fatigues. The next night, at the teams' steak fry at an establishment called Rawhide, Hurricanes defensive tackle Jerome Brown directed the military withdrawal: "We're not here for you all to make monkeys of us. We're here to make war. Did the Japanese sit down with Pearl Harbor before they bombed? Let's go."

Miami blabbed. Penn State clammed up. The battle lines were oversimplified: Evil vs. good, style vs. substance, "Miami Vice" vs. "Father Knows Best."

Come the Fiesta Bowl night, the Hurricanes were still talking trash — during pregame warmups. "They were such a bunch of jerks," Bauer recalls.

Penn State was ready for them.

"Giving Joe and his staff that much time (41 days)? It was a

THE VICE PRESIDENT
WASHINGTON, D.C. 20501

[signature: Geo Bush]
VICE PRESIDENT

Paterno offers to coach if right Gipper is found

Never mind being No. 1 in football, Joe Paterno has other things on his mind. He'd like to coach someone into the nation's No. 1 office.

"I would really like to find somebody and help them become president of the United States," said the coach of No. 2-rated Penn State.

Other Paterno thoughts:

■ On paying players: "Maybe $50 a month, because if a kid doesn't have a couple of bucks in his pocket it's tough to be in the main scheme of campus life."

■ Players participating in other campus activities: "(Former player) Mike Reid had the lead in *Guys and Dolls* and I loved it. To have one of our kids run for undergraduate president would be great."

■ The overemphasis on winning: "College presidents fire coaches that don't win enough games. Take (former Texas coach) Fred Akers, he wins and they fire him. A lot of guys say they (presidents) are not going to get me (fired), 'I'm going to cheat.'"

Mr. Joe Paterno
Head Coach
Penn State University
State College, Pennsylvania 16802

Dec. 21, 1986

Dear Joe —

Keep me in mind!
(see attached clip)
Merry Christmas and Happy 1987. I'm sure proud of you — Geo

A page from Paterno's scrapbook shows George Bush's invitation to coach him to the presidency. Paterno accepted his offer, seconding his nomination at the 1988 Republican National Convention in New Orleans. Above, Paterno at the convention with Pa. Sen. John Heinz.

no-brainer," Bauer adds. Defensive coordinator Jerry Sandusky came up with 150 different defenses. "I called the defensive signals; it was bananas. But we had a group of guys who had played for three years. So he could put guys in different coverages, blitzes, schemes. Miami never saw anything like that."

Miami quarterback Vinny Testaverde, the Heisman Trophy winner and eventual No. 1 NFL draft choice, tossed five interceptions that night — including the fate-sealing one to Pete Giftopoulos at the Penn State 1 with seconds remaining.

"Testaverde, after that game, was shell-shocked. I don't think he recovered for 10 years," Bauer says.

The Lions, after scaling the mountain for that 14-10 triumph, never fully recovered, either. They never reached such rarefied air the rest of the decade.

"1987 was very similar to '83," Bauer recalls. "The year after

a national championship, you don't have enough good guys coming back."

Blair Thomas arose to rush for 1,414 yards in '87, helping the Lions to an 8-3 record and a Citrus Bowl berth. But he injured a knee during pre-bowl workouts and, a month later, underwent surgery that would sideline him for all of 1988.

There followed another Paterno plummet — at 5-6 his worst ever and Penn State's first losing season in half a century. And, no, Paterno wasn't an assistant the last time that happened, back in that 3-4-1 season of '38. The Lions of '88 lost four of their final five games, and by a collective 104-60. Just like the old days.

The "Hellfires of '88" the coach later called the season in his autobiography, "Paterno: By the Book." He went through three kickers and four quarterbacks that year. In the end, he mostly used Tony Sacca, the first true freshman to play quarterback under Paterno. The Thomas-less team could hardly budge. As Paterno admitted afterward, "A lot of people smelled the kill against us."

"There was too much complaining on offense," recalls

Brian Chizmar, a linebacker then. "And how the heck did we lose to Rutgers (21-16 in Game 3)? I just think we had a lot of people who thought they were better than they were."

Had Paterno lost it?

Had we heard that enough yet ('79, '83)?

Once again, Paterno rolled up his sleeves and pant cuffs. Once again, he cleared his busy social calendar. He talked about being more of a hands-on coach. You can't get much more hands-on than a 62-year-old coach standing atop a two-man blocking sled.

"It's not to say he was ever not committed," Chizmar remembers. "But he demanded more (after '88). He expected more. That was also a time when the personalities of players started changing. You had to recruit a lot more bigger egos that you had to massage."

Ever adept, Paterno adapted once again.

"That's what makes you successful: you have to adapt to the times," Chizmar continues.

The '89 season brought vexing times as well. Quarterback Tom Bill underwent counseling for an alcohol problem. Once he returned, he and Sacca continued to shuttle at quarterback. Thomas, after his one-year recovery from knee surgery, carried the team: He constituted 40 percent of the Lions' offense and dropped the ball only once in the 329 times he touched it. Penn State beat Brigham Young in a wild Holiday Bowl, 50-39, but only after Gary Brown returned an interception 53 yards for a touchdown with 45 seconds left.

"You hope that you're not part of teams that sometimes go awry," says Chizmar, whose career started as a freshman on that championship team, and kind of went downhill from there. "But I like to think that in '89 we came back to set the tone for the future teams, back to what it's all about."

That same December brought news of a change for the next decade. Penn State, long an independent, a college-football orphan, was set to enter the prestigious Big Ten Conference. That was enough of a new mountain for Paterno to stick around a while longer.

"I think he's said to every recruiting class since 1980 that, 'I'm going to be here five more years.' He'll be there forever."

SYMBOL OF THE 80's

BOB WHITE

BOB WHITE WAS CONSIDERED Pennsylvania's top high-school prospect the winter of 1982. Pitt, Ohio State, Florida State, Georgia and South Carolina wooed him. Promises and rose petals were sprinkled about his feet.

And Joe Paterno told him to read.

Actually, Joe Paterno told him to seek out Sue Paterno, and to read whatever books she prescribed.

As recruiting pitches go, this was a dandy one, if you were a salesman for the Book of the Month Club.

But White felt at ease with Penn State, with both Paternos, and left behind his foster brother in Freeport, Pa., for his new family in State College.

"It was something of an agreement that Sue and I had worked out on my trips," White recalls. "She and I had this going through my freshman year. She was an instructor or teacher at one time, and we worked together quite a while — on papers and sharing books."

With direction from the Coach's wife, White read Jack London and Charles Dickens novels, he read "The Adventures of Huckleberry Finn" and "The Old Man and the Sea." He became a more than respectable student. When White returned to Penn State as a graduate student, he was a study hall proctor for football and track players. Who would walk in one day to counsel another generation of players but Sue Paterno.

"She's still very involved," White says.

White had been raised in Haines City, Fla., a trying climate for young people — and that wasn't a reference to the heat and humidity. Haines City brims with migratory workers, unemployment, restlessness. The sturdy football player left for bucolic Freeport as a high school sophomore. Stellar junior and senior seasons led him down the recruiting trail, which led him to Penn State and the Paterno reading lists.

He went from a young student who prepared two-page book reports for Sue Paterno to a fifth-year senior defensive end who gathered 17 sacks his final two seasons for Joe Paterno. Aiming to please the Paternos, he did.

White also was among the 16 fifth-year seniors who experienced both the 1982 and 1986 national championships at Penn State and played for a chance to win another in 1985.

The 1984 season, though, was pretty darn tough. Penn State closed with back-to-back losses by a combined 75-18. Paterno sent his players into the offseason remembering one word he used to describe them: "babies."

"When you get a bunch of competitors in a situation like

that, they don't want to stay there," says White, "It doesn't feel good. It doesn't taste good. So that's what motivates you to do better."

White and the Nittany Lions went 11-0 the next season, 1985, and 11-0 the season after that, winning a second national championship with a victory over Miami in the Fiesta Bowl.

"It was a beautiful way to enter as freshmen and to leave as seniors," White says. "You were at the top of the heap. There was no better way to go out."

You couldn't have written it better in a book.

The epilogue to his story: After brief stints with the NFL San Francisco 49ers and Cleveland Browns, White returned to Penn State for graduate school and an administrative position. He worked in the university's admissions office for three years. He worked in the Office of Governmental Affairs, serving as a university representative in Harrisburg, the state capital, for two years. Then he went back to the athletic department, went back to counsel athletes on academics, went back to the place where he could direct young minds.

Much the same way the Paternos did with him a decade before.

— C.F.

SYMBOL OF THE 80's

GREG GATTUSO

MAYBE, JUST MAYBE, Greg Gattuso wasn't the typical kind of recruit for Penn State. For one thing, he grew up a Pitt fan. For another, he wasn't the most pliable, straight-and-narrow fellow Joe Paterno could find.

But Paterno could find him. Even playing hooky from Seton-LaSalle High as a senior one winter day in 1980.

"I'm home all by myself, in my room, the radio blaring," Gattuso recalls of that day. "I hear 'knock, knock, knock' on my door. I open the door, and he's standing there.

"He says, 'You OK?'

"I say, 'Uhhh, yeah. I had a little fever.'

"He checks my temperature with his hand. 'Are you drinking fluids? Take good care of yourself.'"

The burly defensive tackle was widely recruited, but only one coach put his hand to the kid's forehead. Paterno and his staff "were just so intensely honest," Gattuso said. "No promises. They were interested in my education, which, at the time, I didn't care about."

Gattuso entered Penn State after a distressing 1979 season. The coach was taking a more active role with his players, with preparation, with practices. He was so concerned about his players, he refused to let them place themselves in situations where they could sprain an ankle, or worse.

The hands-on Paterno told them to keep off the grass.

"Joe had this fetish of walking on grass. If there was a sidewalk, and you weren't walking on it, he'd scream at you," Gattuso recalls. " 'Gattuso, get off the grass. Get on the sidewalk. What's the matter with you?' In that goofy voice, you know?"

Gattuso listened. Most every member of the Nittany Lions did back then, and they followed Paterno to 10-2 records in 1980 and 1981 and then to the top.

In 1982, the team lost early in the season, at Alabama, and righted itself enough to earn an invitation to play top-ranked Georgia in the Sugar Bowl for the national championship. Four days before the game, Gattuso was benched. Something about "bad posture in a meeting."

"I begged and pleaded and cried, begged and pleaded and cried some more, and chased Joe down the hall," Gattuso recalls. Soon enough the defensive tackle was back with the first team. "I found out later that it was their way of straightening out any problems before they started."

Gattuso made seven tackles that game, including two of Heisman Trophy winner Herschel Walker on carries that netted minus-2 yards. He starred the next season on a team that rallied from an 0-3 start to go 8-1-1 the rest of the way.

The burly defensive tackle tried out with the Washington Redskins, but was cut by July's end, 1984. He returned home to Brookline lost, confused.

"My dad (Steve) kept telling me, 'Call Joe, he'll help you.' I was saying, 'Joe never liked me.' I was always a little mouthy and on the edge. Just kind of a wise-guy character.

"My dad called, and Joe told him, 'Have him up here Monday.' "

Gattuso toiled as a graduate assistant during the fall of 1984. He graduated. He became a jail guard for a while. But something unforeseen grabbed him during that fall of 1984: The notion to coach a team of his own.

"The last thing in the world I ever thought I would be is a coach," Gattuso says.

He returned home to Pittsburgh, where he eventually coached his alma mater, Seton-LaSalle High, to a district championship. He later became head coach at Duquesne University, a Division I-AA non-scholarship program.

Gattuso wound up a college football coach like Paterno.

Funny thing. Now he finds himself uttering Paternoisms to his own Duquesne players.

"Get off the grass. What's the matter with you?"—

C.F.

CHAPTER SIX

BY RON COOK

———

J OE PATERNO IS A LUCKY MAN. He has spent a lifetime in college athletics and he has only one regret. Can you imagine that? Just one regret?

OK, so maybe regret isn't quite the right word. "I don't want you to think for a second that I'm not happy about being in the Big Ten because that isn't the case," Paterno said. "I can't imagine anything being better for Penn State than the Big Ten. What happened turned out for the best for us."

Still, Paterno admits to feeling a sense of disappointment. As wonderful as the Big Ten-Penn State marriage is, it never would have happened if his vision for an all-sports conference in the East had come to fruition. "That could have been something special, something really great for all of us, geographically and competitively," Paterno said.

This goes back to the early 1980's. Paterno dreamed of an eight-school super conference of Penn State, Pitt, Syracuse, West Virginia, Boston College, Temple, Rutgers and Maryland. His plan collapsed in 1982 when Pitt joined the Big East, a powerful, money-making, television-friendly basketball conference that had formed in 1979 with Syracuse and Boston College among the seven original members.

"It was a bitter pill for me to swallow," Paterno says. People close to him will tell you he has never forgiven Pitt for this slight. Pitt officials have called him a hypocrite on more than one occasion. They love to point out that Penn State applied for membership to the Big East and was rejected long before Pitt joined the basketball league.

And what does Paterno say? "That whole thing is one of my greatest disappointments. I think there were some short-sighted people involved at the time. We could have been so far ahead of the rest of the pack in college athletics. That's what I feel bad about. I feel bad about what might have been."

The dream died a painful death for Paterno. Even after Pitt went with the Big East, he hoped he could persuade Pitt or Syracuse to leave the conference to join him in building a new, all-sports league. He figured if he could convince one, the other surely would follow. So would Boston College. He had spoken with Maryland officials, who had led him to believe they would be willing to leave the Atlantic Coast Conference to join an Eastern League.

Dave Gavitt, the Big East commissioner at the time, knew all this. He fought hard to keep his league together.

"I flew to Hartford and met with Gavitt," Paterno says. "He said, 'We'd want you in the Big East for basketball.' I said, 'Penn State does not want to be in a basketball conference. We want to get into a sports conference.'

"We already were in a basketball conference (the Atlantic 10) and that wasn't working out. Our other sports teams needed to be in a conference. I'm talking about a conference where each school is there for each other, helping each other out in all sports.

"My idea just didn't work out."

Syracuse stayed in the Big East. "Their guy (Athletic Director Jake Crouthamel) is the guy who really squashed the Eastern conference," Paterno says. "People don't realize that he and Gavitt were roommates at Dartmouth."

Pitt also elected to stay in the Big East. "You'd have to ask their people, but I think, because I was the athletic director and football coach at the time, that was a problem for them. I think, in their mind, they might have thought we would have dominated the conference."

As the 1990's approached, Paterno knew he and Penn

State were quickly running out of time. The Nittany Lions had been playing football as an independent since 1887. They were enormously successful, especially under Paterno, who became head coach in 1966 and took a 289-74-3 record into the 1997 season.

"In the last 25 years, Syracuse beat us three times," Paterno said in 1993. "Pitt beat us six times. Rutgers beat us once. Temple did not beat us. Boston College beat us twice. Maryland did not beat us. . . .

"No matter how good you think you are and how loyal your fans are, there's got to be a reason to come see a game. If you're not playing for the national championship, you've got problems. If that's the only thing you've got going and you're not playing for a league championship and you don't

Paterno is escorted off the field after the Nittany Lions upset No. 1 Notre Dame 24-21 in South Bend on Nov. 17, 1990.

have significant competition, you can only beat up on people for so long.

"That's why I got everybody together and said, 'We've got to make up our minds about what we're going to do around here. We've got to get ourselves in a conference. Why don't we try the Big Ten?'

"We all thought it was a long shot, but we got lucky. The head of the Big Ten presidents (Stanley Ikenberry at Illinois) really carried the ball for us."

Dr. Bryce Jordan, the Penn State president, began serious talks with Big Ten officials in May 1989 about joining the conference. "The idea has interested me since I became president seven years ago," he said at the time. "Penn State is a Big Ten-type institution. Academically, we're more in line with the mission of the Big Ten schools than we are with certain Eastern institutions."

Ikenberry was intrigued with the possibilities. He said Penn State's appeal to the Big Ten was academics. He said Penn State shared many of the conference's views toward academic reform in intercollegiate athletics, such as higher entrance requirements for athletes, freshman ineligibility and the shortening of spring football and the basketball season.

Ikenberry was the right guy for Penn State to have in its corner. He was able to convince the other Big Ten presidents that adding Penn State made sense. At a news conference on Dec. 19, 1989, he announced that an agreement had been reached for Penn State to become the 11th member of the Big Ten. It became official on June 4, 1990.

Penn State's move changed college athletics. Universities everywhere rushed to join a conference. In 1991, the Big East Football Conference was formed with Pitt, Syracuse, Miami, Boston College, West Virginia, Rutgers, Temple and Virginia Tech. By then, Paterno had moved on to what he has called "bigger and better things."

It was a humbled Paterno, who, at that press conference in December 1989, said, "I'm very excited about this. After being at this institution for 40 years — from the time it was a cow college before it was a university — I'd very much like to have the chance to compete for a Rose Bowl. It's a little bit of an ego thing, but it's something I would really like to do."

Paterno accomplished that goal in 1994 when Penn State won the Big Ten championship. It beat Oregon in the Rose Bowl to complete a 12-0 season. As proud as Paterno is of that title, he said he is happier about what the Big Ten has meant to Penn State as a university. "The momentum we've built up since we've joined the conference is incredible."

That's financial momentum.

Paterno predicts that Penn State will raise between $600 million and $1 billion in the next five years from its alumni association, the largest of its kind in America. Much of that money will flow in because of Paterno himself.

All of Penn State's 29 sports teams will benefit. A $13.8-million football complex is being built. More than $55 million has been budgeted for a variety of projects, including a new natatorium, indoor track facility, fitness center and sports hall of fame. Still to come within three or four years is an expansion of 93,967-seat Beaver Stadium by 10,000 to 12,000 to accommodate the amazing demand for football tickets. The Nittany Lions drew 62,000 to their Blue & White spring game in 1997. "I don't think there's any question we have to do something," Paterno says. "Our young alumni have such a tough time getting tickets. That isn't fair to them."

The Penn State men's and women's basketball programs are in a beautiful new home because of their Big Ten membership. Plans to build the spectacular Bryce Jordan Center were hastened after the school joined the conference. The $55 million arena, which seats 15,300 for basketball and 16,000 for other events, opened in January 1996.

"I used to think we had good facilities until I saw what Michigan and Ohio State and Michigan State and Wisconsin had," Paterno says. "I mean, ours are good, but they're not state of the art. Our people don't want to be second-class citizens in the Big Ten Conference. It's easy to sell them on making donations to the university when you tell them your goal is to be the best in the Big Ten."

Being in the high-profile conference also has helped the Penn State sports teams from a competition standpoint. That's especially true of the men's basketball program. Former Pitt Coach Roy Chipman predicted as much in 1989 when he heard the Nittany Lions were joining the Big Ten. He knew what Big East membership had done for his program. "The Big Ten is going to open a lot of doors for Penn State," Chipman said. "They'll be able to recruit kids in the Midwest who want to stay in the Big Ten. They'll be able to recruit kids in California and tell them their folks will be able to watch them on television 12 or 13 times a year. They'll be able to sell that conference."

The Penn State men's basketball team finished in second

place in the Big Ten in 1995-96 and went to the NCAA Tournament. It slipped to a 10-17 record in 1996-97, but Paterno said, "It's only going to be a matter of time until they get it going and keep it going. I think we'll be good forever in basketball unless we really get sloppy." Added Chipman, "I really believe, because of the Big Ten, Penn State basketball might finally reach the same level as its football program."

That will take some doing, of course. Paterno has continued his phenomenal success since joining the Big Ten, overcoming numerous predictions of gloom and doom along the way. *Sports Illustrated,* for one, in a 1993 story headlined "Unhappy Days in Happy Valley," identified the Big East as the football conference on the rise and predicted Penn State's recruiting would suffer because Eastern kids don't want to play against Midwestern teams.

That just hasn't been the case. Some recruiting gurus ranked Penn State's recruiting classes in 1996 and 1997 as the best in the country. All had them in the top five. "It didn't make any sense," Paterno said of the dire forecasting. "It wasn't as if we were moving the university to Alaska. I think in the long run, going into the Big Ten will help our recruiting, not only here in the East but everywhere. It has tremendous exposure."

Not everyone in the Big Ten welcomed the Penn State football team with open arms. The marriage was struck quickly on the presidential level, meaning the athletic directors and coaches weren't consulted. The AD's were insulted. The coaches were fearful of adding a loss to their schedules. "Penn State will make our jobs harder," former Michigan Coach Gary Moeller said. Added Iowa Coach Hayden Fry, "They'll injure people and maybe cost somebody a national championship."

Paterno said he wasn't surprised by the chilly reception. "If I had been in their shoes and I wasn't consulted, I'd resent it, too. Plus, there was going to be an attitude on their part of, 'Hey, who are these guys? Do think they're hot shots who are going to come in and dominate the conference? No way.' There was going to be a lot of fighting for Big Ten pride against Penn State. We weren't one of the guys yet. Anybody who didn't understand that doesn't understand competi-

tion."

Just how ridiculous was it? "We're not allowed to say 'Penn State,' " Michigan recruit Jon Ritchie once said. He's a Pennsylvania kid from Cumberland Valley who got away from Paterno. "We have to say, 'The other team,' or 'The 11th school.' "

Penn State earned its respect on the field. It went 6-2 against Big Ten teams in 1993, its first season in the conference, and probably would have gone to the Rose Bowl if not for a tremendous goal-line stand by Michigan in a 21-13 loss. In their dream season of 1994, the Nittany Lions beat their eight league opponents by an average of 27 points and whacked Ohio State, 63-14. They finished third in the conference in 1995 and 1996. And they went into 1997 not just as the team to beat in the Big Ten, but as the nation's No. 1-ranked team. It was the first time a Paterno team was ranked No. 1 in the preseason.

"The competition in the conference, from top to bottom, has been much tougher than I thought it was going to be," Paterno said. "The Big Ten was a great league long before we got there."

Paterno said the Rose Bowl experience was everything he imagined it would be, even if it didn't please all the Penn State fans. The Nittany Lions crushed Oregon, 38-20, but still finished No. 2 in the national polls behind unbeaten Nebraska, which defeated Miami in the Orange Bowl. Some Penn State loyalists argued that, if the team still had been an independent, it could have played a better, higher-ranked team in a bowl and won Paterno's third national championship.

"It's like I told our squad," Paterno said. "We did something no Penn State team has ever done. We won all our games, went to the Rose Bowl and won it. That's not all bad. We can't sit around and mope about what might have been."

Penn State fans should be able to avoid that kind of disappointment once the Big Ten, the Pacific 10 Conference and the Rose Bowl join the bowl alliance in 1998. Paterno lobbied for that change. He long has been an advocate of a national college football playoffs. "Can you imagine what it would have been like if we had played Nebraska in '94? Two great

programs? My God, and they talk about everything that's wrong with college sports. We could have played that game before 150 million people. We could have easily made $100 million. Then, we could have turned around and used that money to help solve the gender-equity problem."

The biggest complaint Paterno hears from the Penn State fans these days is predictable. "It's always the same thing: 'Why can't we play Syracuse?' 'Why can't we play West Virginia?' 'Why can't we get Pitt on the schedule forever?' That's the one thing that's hurt us. We can't play everyone our people want us to play."

Penn State began playing West Virginia in 1904, Syracuse in 1922. Neither school is on the Nittany Lions' schedule now. The Penn State-Pitt series goes back to 1893. It resumed in 1997 after a four-year hiatus — Pitt probably wishes it hadn't because Penn State won, 34-17 — but no games between the two are scheduled after the 2000 season.

Paterno pettiness has been blamed for the interruptions of the great rivalries. His critics say that he holds a grudge against Pitt and Syracuse because they would not form an Eastern conference and West Virginia because it wanted to immediately expel Penn State from the Atlantic 10 once it became clear the Lions were Big Ten-bound.

In addition, Paterno never has hid the fact he resents Syracuse for refusing to play Penn State in men's basketball. Once, he got into a nasty public hissing contest with long-time Syracuse Coach Jim Boeheim, who had said Penn State would never be able to recruit successfully in basketball because of its location. "What's he talking about?" Paterno asked. "Obviously, he can't win. He can't win a national championship with the best material in the country, year-in, year-out."

Allied against Paterno was former Pitt Athletic Director Ed Bozik, who, in 1991, said, "It's unfortunate that someone would let personal relationships interfere with the series. The fans, alumni and players didn't want it to end. It was personal, petty vindictiveness."

Paterno said revenge isn't a factor when he sets Penn State's football schedule. He reacted angrily when he was criticized for temporarily halting the Pitt series. "I've been at Penn State a long time. I hope, that with all the effort I've put in here, I am not getting senile or petty that I'm going to hurt this program just to get even with somebody. That's got absolutely nothing to do with it."

Paterno said Penn State has scheduling problems because it must play eight Big Ten games — four at home and four on the road. He said Penn State needs to play intersectional games. "I want to do what I think is best for all of our alumni, not just the ones who live in Western Pennsylvania. We're a national institution. Our alumni want us to go into the Southwest. They want us in the Southeast once in a while. They want us on the West Coast once in a while. We have to try to do that."

Paterno said Penn State also needs six home games each year to support its vast athletic program. He gladly would be willing to play Pitt, Syracuse or West Virginia if one was willing to come to Beaver Stadium two times out of every three years. (Bozik responded in 1991, "We're not going to take second-class status to anyone.")

Paterno celebrates Penn State's 38-20 victory over the University of Oregon in the Rose Bowl game at Pasadena, Calif., on Jan. 2, 1995.

"To say I operate out of spite is wrong," Paterno says. "I'm not anti-anybody. I'm a college football guy whose obligation is to do what's best for Penn State. That's who's paying me. I just feel bad that some people aren't more sympathetic."

Paterno says he wishes Pitt, Syracuse and West Virginia well. "I'm not like some people. I think the Big East is a very viable conference."

It's easy for Paterno to be so magnanimous. He knows he still has the top college football program in the East even though he plays in a Midwestern conference. Why should he look down his nose at the Big East? Enough other people will do if for him. They will tell you an Eastern football league without Penn State is really no league at all.

THE JOURNEY CONTINUES

CHAPTER SEVEN

BY RON COOK

———

EVERYBODY IN COLLEGE FOOTBALL was watching what was happening at Notre Dame. This was after the 1996 season. Lou Holtz resigned as Irish coach after 11 seasons, 100 victories and a national championship in 1988. The most glamorous coaching position in the game was available. All Notre Dame had to do was ask and the lucky man would come running.

The search took Notre Dame to Evanston, Ill., where Gary Barnett had quickly turned around a Northwestern program that had endured 20 consecutive losing seasons. Four years into Barnett's tenure, in 1995, the Wildcats won the Big Ten championship and played in the Rose Bowl. They shared the league title again in 1996 and went to the Citrus Bowl.

Barnett was arguably the hottest name in college coaching. He was the logical choice for Notre Dame. There was only one problem. Barnett said he didn't want the job.

"I wasn't surprised," said Joe Paterno, a particularly interested observer.

Not surprised? That a Northwestern man turned down Notre Dame?

"I really wasn't," Paterno said. "I think all coaches want to feel like they can make a difference somewhere. Gary's success at Northwestern has helped that university in so many ways. The pride he's brought to the school, the prestige, the money he's been able to raise, what he's been able to do with their facilities . . . Gary Barnett is making a difference at Northwestern. There's no way he could have that kind of impact at Notre Dame."

The story says a lot about Barnett, but it says more about Paterno. It explains Paterno's unwavering loyalty to Penn State. The 1997 season is his 48th in Happy Valley, his 32nd as head coach. His first 16 were as assistant to Rip Engle.

"They ask me what I'd like written about me when I'm gone," Paterno says. "I hope they write I made Penn State a better place, not just that I was a good football coach."

That's Paterno's legacy, not his epitaph. At 70, his work is far from finished. "I want to go five more years," he says.

That would give Paterno a chance to reach a number of personal goals. He loathes talking about them, but they are no secret. He would like to coach at Penn State for at least 50 years. He would like to break the great Bear Bryant's Division I record of 323 victories. And he would like to win his third national championship.

"Obviously, all those things would be nice if they happened," Paterno says. It does not seem impossible. As the 1997 season began, Paterno's record was 289-74-3 and the Nittany Lions were ranked the nation's No. 1 team.

"But to be very frank, I give it very little thought. If it doesn't happen, what's the difference? My biggest concern is that those things will become a distraction to the squad. It's like my old boss, Rip Engle, used to say in our meetings, 'It's not our team. It's their team. We're getting paid to help them become the best they want to be.' The players are important, not me."

Five more years also would give Paterno the opportunity to raise more money for Penn State. He has been a vice chairman of the $352 million Campaign for Penn State and was a committee member for a $20 million effort toward building the Bryce Jordan Center, the university's multipurpose arena. He personally raised $15 million toward the new $27 million Paterno Library, which will open in 1998 as an extension of Pattee Library. ("A great university starts with a great library," he has always said.)

Now, Paterno will play a major role on the steering committee in Penn State's most extensive fund-raising effort, which he predicts will raise between $600 million and $1 billion in the next five years.

"I've always taken great pride in this whole university, not just the football team," Paterno said. "I've always believed if you don't march together, you're not going to be very successful. We've done that here. Anybody who comes on this campus and looks around can sense the vibrancy right now."

No one can take more credit than Paterno. He has given a

Penn State commencement address, received four honorary degrees, testified before Congress and given a seconding speech at the Republican National Convention. He turned down a chance to run for governor of Pennsylvania. He wanted to stay at Penn State. He wanted to make a difference.

Paterno's record speaks for itself. Twelve seasons of at least 11 victories. Twenty Top Ten finishes. National championships in 1982 and 1986 and his undefeated but uncrowned teams in 1968, 1969, 1973 and 1994. A bowl record of 18-8-1, the best in history. More than 200 players he has sent to the NFL, including 22 first-round draft choices. Coach of the Year honors an unprecedented four times. His selection as *Sports Illustrated's* Sportsman of the Year in 1986.

Is it most remarkable that Paterno has done all that at one university? At the start of the 1997 season, he had been involved in exactly half of the 1,044 games Penn State had played since 1887. He had many opportunities to leave for higher-paying coaching jobs but came close only once, in 1973, when Billy Sullivan offered him a share of the New England Patriots to entice him to coach the team.

"I actually took that job," Paterno said. "I went to bed that night, I was committed to Billy Sullivan. But you know, it just wasn't right. I got up about three o'clock in the morning, woke up Sue, and said, 'I'm not going to take that job.' She started to cry. She didn't want to go. She'd never let me know that. It wasn't the money. Coming from a family that never owned a house, to think that I was going to own part of the Patriots really meant something. It would have started off at 2 or 3 percent, but then I could have worked myself up to 10 or 12 percent.

"But everything went back to what you want out of life. We were happy at Penn State. So I called Billy back and said, 'Look, I'm sorry.' That was one of the toughest calls I've ever had to make. All I think about now is how lucky I was to say no. I couldn't have had a better life anywhere else."

Or is it most amazing that Paterno has been so successful for so long while dealing with 18- to 22-year-old men? His love for the opera and classical music has never changed. But his players have gone from listening to rock-and-roll to hard rock to rap to hip-hop to whatever it is young people listen to these days.

"I don't think he's really changed much from the time I first met him," Jack Ham said. He played linebacker at Penn State from 1968-70 and went on to star for the Pittsburgh Steelers. He paid Paterno the ultimate tribute by asking him to be his presenter at his induction to the Pro Football Hall of Fame.

"No one did more for me, not just in football but in all facets of life, than Joe," Ham said.

"When you're 18 and going to college, you can end up in a lot of different directions. But he immediately gets your feet on the ground. Priorities were always the big thing with him. Family is first. Education is second. Football is third. That never changed. I think that's sometimes why he took more pride in his players who went on to become successful businessmen or orthopedic surgeons or whatever than he did in those who played pro football.

"He's still the same disciplinarian. He'll still bench a kid or read him the riot act. He still won't tolerate any of that silly garbage you see in the end zone. The kids playing for him are lucky. I know I was lucky. I never would have made it if not for the confidence and maturity I came away with after being with him for four years."

Paterno really hasn't changed. You should have heard him on Media Day in 1997 when he announced one of his top wide receivers, junior Corey Jones, was academically ineligible for the season after skipping some Spanish classes and flunking the

Paterno has won his share of honors over the years, but a still-greater prize remains: Alabama Coach Paul (Bear) Bryant's mark of 323 victories.

course. "I'm disappointed in him and he should be disappointed in himself. He let himself down and his family down. The No. 1 reason he's here is to get an education. Forget No. 2. Until he takes care of No. 1, there never will be a No. 2."

Is it any wonder that the most recent NCAA statistics showed that the Penn State football program had a four-year 80 percent graduation rate compared to a 53 percent national average? That Penn State's graduation rate for African-American football players was 81 percent compared to a 43 percent national average? That Paterno has produced 20 first-team Academic All-Americas, 13 Hall of Fame Scholar-Athletes and 16 NCAA post-graduate scholarship winners?

Despite that rewarding success, Paterno says someone would have to be "nuts" to go into coaching today. "It is just so demanding. People expect you to be Moses." He blames the media and fans for what he calls the "instant gratification syndrome." The exposure and salaries have increased so much that a coach needs to win big and win quickly to not be considered a failure.

The players, Paterno says, are not to blame. "They're better today than they used to be. They're not phonies. They're not hypocrites, most of them," Paterno told *The American Enterprise Magazine* in 1996. "They've had to survive a much tougher situation. I don't know how some of these kids handle it. The kind of money that's out there, the agents who are out there, the girls . . . I mean, I have to chase girls away from the locker room some nights. All the tough decisions in my life when I was a kid, until I left high school, were made by my church or my family. I mean, I didn't have any choices whether I wanted to sleep with a girl or do anything like that, God forbid.

"We've put the kids today in a tough environment where they've got to make a lot of tough decisions and they've got to work their way through it on their own. I think they respond better.

"The problem is not the kids, the problem is us. The kids need somebody whom they trust and somebody who's honest. They look at the political scene out there today . . . Who wouldn't get disillusioned? For crying out loud, they've got to be sick about it. It's going to be their country. I think the fact that they haven't had a revolution speaks well for them."

Paterno is careful about the type of player he recruits to Penn

State. He has had his share of players who have driven drunk, burglarized apartments or assaulted fellow students, but for the most part, you can see a difference between his players and those at other major powers. His players generally make a better appearance in the post-game interviews. They talk better, represent their university better.

"That's why I was so happy when Penn State beat Miami to win the national championship in '86," Ham says. "Those were two diametrically opposed programs. One said, 'I'm going to bring in any renegade to win.' The other said, 'I'm going to win the right way with good people.'"

"I don't want to say our kids are better," says Fran Ganter, Penn State's long-time offensive coordinator, "but I will say we spend a great deal of time evaluating character. Joe always has the final say. He likes to meet the parents. He'll ask us, 'What did the principal say about the kid?' We'll say, 'We didn't talk to the principal. We talked to the coaches.' He'll say, 'Go back and talk to the principal. Talk to the classmates.' He wants to know everything."

That's one explanation for Ganter's spending a lifetime at Penn State. The 1997 season was his 27th on Paterno's staff, his 31st in Happy Valley if you count his days as a student-athlete. Former Penn State center Bucky Greeley once said of Ganter, "His parents dropped him off and forgot to pick him up."

Greeley also could have been talking about defensive coordinator Jerry Sandusky (30 years as a Paterno assistant), quarterbacks coach Dick Anderson (21 years) and secondary coach Tom Bradley (19 years). "The Supreme Court has more turnover than the Penn State football staff," Ham says. The coaches have stayed for more reasons than just the atmosphere in State College, agreeable as that is.

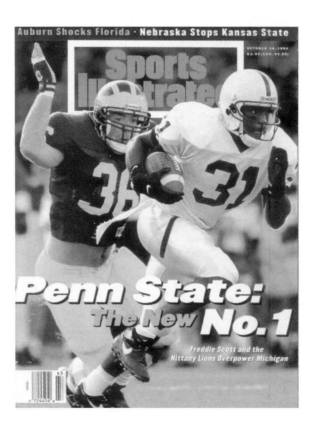

Freddie Scott and the
Nittany Lions Overpower Michigan

"We think we're working with the best young men in America," Ganter says. "We're also working for THE coach."

As rigid as Paterno can be, he has proven to be flexible. Never was that more apparent than after the 1992 season. Penn State was 5-0 that year when it lost at home to No. 2 Miami, 17-14. It finished with a 7-5 record after getting blown out by Bill Walsh's Stanford team, 24-3, in the Blockbuster Bowl. There was only one coaching genius on the sideline that afternoon — and it wasn't Paterno.

That season, Penn State lacked discipline on the field, played horrendous defense, kicked erratically and ineffectively shuffled quarterbacks John Sacca, Wally Richardson and Kerry Collins. Off the field, the program was just as miserable. A gaggle of players was arrested. Some moaned about Paterno. Others pointed fingers at each other. Happy Valley wasn't so happy.

That wasn't the first time critics suggested the game had passed Paterno by. Penn State went 6-5 in 1984, only to come back in 1985 to go 11-1 and lose in the national championship game to Oklahoma in the Orange Bowl, then win the title in 1986. And the 1988 team finished 5-6, the first and only losing season at Penn State since 1938. The Nittany Lions came back in 1989 to go 8-3-1 and beat Brigham Young in the Holiday Bowl.

But early in 1993, the wolves really howled at Paterno. Unflattering comparisons were made to Bryant, who was headed toward another national championship in 1982 until he lost at Tennessee at midseason. Then he lost to Louisiana State. And Southern Mississippi. And Auburn. Bryant retired after that season. At 69, he had exhausted his supply of miracles. Even Paterno wondered if Bear hadn't stayed too long. Now, people were wondering that about him.

"I always felt like we knew what we were doing," Paterno says. "When I don't feel that way, I'll get out of it, I really will. But, at the same time, you had to be pretty dumb not to sense that something was wrong. I guess I just felt with that '92 team that our pride and our tradition would carry us and everything would take care of itself. Obviously, that wasn't the case. We got careless and sloppy. I didn't know what was going on with the squad. I had lost contact with the kids. That embarrassed me. That's as bad as I felt about our program since I came here."

Give Paterno credit. When the 1992 season ended, he met individually with the seniors and asked for their evaluations of him and the program. They were brutally honest. They told Paterno he cared too much about other things — politics, solving the game's evils, being a football god — and not enough about his team. They told him he was distant, arrogant. They told him he was a tyrant, unapproachable, uninterested in their input.

All of this was confirmed in a book about Penn State football, "For the Glory." Ken Denlinger, a Washington Post writer and a friend of Paterno's, was given complete access to follow the recruiting class of 1988, most of which left after the 1992 season. His observations were telling. "The Paterno (whom recruits) had been drawn to on television, the Paterno who had charmed them and their parents, the Paterno who had enthralled much of the country with his wit and enlightened thinking about big-time sport was not the Paterno they were now seeing up close and very personally," Denlinger wrote. "This Paterno was a screamer. The calm voice that had inflated their egos several months before was very quickly cutting to the core of their self-esteem."

This was not the coach or person Paterno wanted to be. Immediately, he established a once-a-week breakfast council

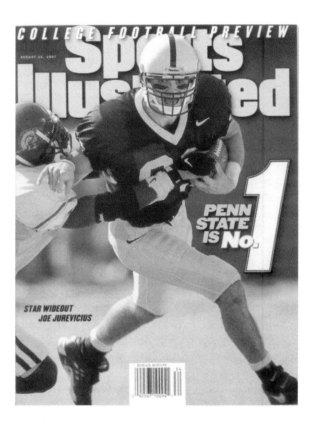

COLLEGE FOOTBALL PREVIEW

Sports Illustrated

AUGUST 25, 1997

PENN STATE IS No. 1

STAR WIDEOUT
JOE JUREVICIUS

with his players. Two from each class were selected by their classmates to meet with the coach at 7:15 on Wednesday mornings. He asked about their problems and listened to their suggestions. He explained why the coaching staff did what it did.

"We've been able to bridge the communication gap," said Collins, Penn State's quarterback at the time. "As a result, I think everyone is willing to put more in the program."

Paterno, eager to redeem himself and energized by Penn State's first season in the Big Ten Conference, led the Nittany Lions to a 10-2 record and No. 8 ranking in 1993. The next year, he enjoyed a dream season. He had one of the best offenses in college football history, led by future No. 1 draft picks Collins, Ki-Jana Carter, Kyle Brady, Jeff Hartings and Andre Johnson. Penn State went 12-0, beat Oregon in the Rose Bowl and finished No. 2 in the national polls. Fans will go to their graves convinced that the Lions, not Nebraska, should have been ranked No. 1.

No one was saying the game had passed Paterno by any longer.

He says he'll know when it's time to quit. "It'll be time when I can't go in a locker room where we're behind at halftime and get myself to rise to the occasion, when I can't do the little things you have to do to get yourself ready, when I can't get up at 5 o'clock in the morning sometimes because you're not settled on some things."

Obviously, that time hasn't come yet.

"Joe still will run gassers with the team, occasionally, if you can believe that," Bradley says.

"He's so sharp physically and mentally that he never misses anything," Ham says. "I can remember when Ganter and I played and Ganter made a mistake about 70 yards away on the practice field. Joe saw it and corrected it."

"He still does that," Ganter says.

"It must be those Coke-bottle glasses," Ham says, grinning.

Paterno might have done his best coaching job in 1996. That team was beaten at Ohio State, 38-7, then lost at home to Iowa, 21-20, two weeks later. The turning point came the following week at Indiana, where the Nittany Lions trailed, 20-10, at halftime. Paterno had benched Richardson, his quarterback, for backup Mike McQueary in the second quarter. Now, he was addressing his squad at halftime.

"Five years I've been here and I've never seen him like that," tight end Keith Olsommer said. "He came right out and said we weren't tough enough to play in the Big Ten. He said he was glad he didn't have to go into a back alley with any of us because he'd be the only one fighting."

Duly challenged, the Nittany Lions scored 38 second-half points to win, 48-26. The week after that, with Richardson back in charge, they pummeled Northwestern, 34-9. Two weeks later, they went to Michigan and won, 29-17, then finished the regular season by beating Michigan State, 32-29.

It was a typical Paterno team, one that gets better as the season progresses. His career record in November games is an astounding 89-22-2. The 1996 team ended its season with a 38-15 beating of Texas in the Fiesta Bowl. It finished No. 7 in the final Associated Press poll with an 11-2 record.

"We do not jump around even though we get a lot of pressure from the media at times and from fans to try different things," Paterno said, explaining his late-season success. "We get better because we don't panic. We just stick with what we know how to do and know how to teach."

The 1996 season was enough to make you think Paterno might coach forever. He knows better. He has talked about "five more years" every year since 1982, but he knows this almost certainly will be the last cycle.

What quest will lie ahead for Paterno? Retirement? More victories?

Paterno's 1997 and 1998 squads both went 9-3 and his 1999 Lion's improved to 10-3 — all good years, but Paterno and Penn State fans wanted more.

During the 2000 season, Paterno will most likely break Paul (Bear) Bryant's record as major college football's winningest coach.

"I think about it" — the end, retirement, his successor, all of it — "all the time. I think about Darrell Royal at Texas. The year after he retired, Texas went undefeated. I asked him, 'Did you know they were going to be so good?' He said, "Joe, the University of Texas has been awfully good to me. I wanted to leave some meat on the bone.'

"That's how I feel here. I've always believed that if you leave the program in good shape, a new, young guy can come in and do it even better. I look at Nebraska. As good a coach as Bob Devaney was, Tom Osborne has been even better. I want that to be the case at Penn State."

That's why Paterno is working so hard on recruiting — "I'm out there more now than I've ever been" — and fund-raising. He wants to make Penn State's sports facilities "state of the art" before he leaves.

"I'm so afraid of us slipping. You get a little careless. You cut some corners. You let up a little. It's like Jerry Kramer wrote in his book after the Packers finally started to lose. He called it, 'Death by Inches.' You take a little off here and a little off there and then, one day, you wake up and you're not as good as the next guy."

That thought isn't all that frightens Paterno. He's afraid of the unknown — life without football. Truth be told, he's afraid of dying. He knows Bryant was dead only a few months after he retired.

"Absolutely, I think about that," Paterno said. "I know I've got to figure out what I want to do with the rest of my life. I don't have a lot of hobbies other than family. I like to read. I enjoy walking, music, the theater. But I've got to find something that will turn me on when I get up in the morning. I need to really think that retirement thing through."

Paterno will delay retirement as long as possible. When that sad day — not just for him, but for college football — finally comes, he wants to help name his successor and hopes it's someone on his staff. It doesn't really matter if it's Ganter — the heir apparent — or Bradley or someone else. The man who gets the coveted Penn State job will be left to ask himself the same hard questions new Notre Dame Coach Bob Davie faced in South Bend.

"How do I make this a better place? How can I possibly make a difference?"

153

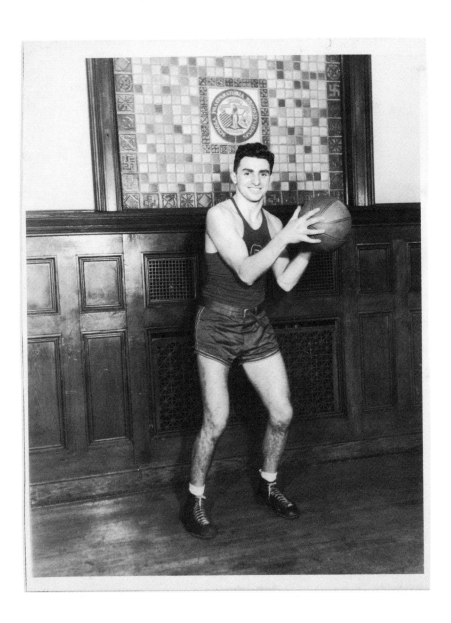

"JUST WINNING IS

"THE PURPOSE OF COLLEGE FOOTBALL IS TO SERVE EDUCATION, NOT THE OTHER WAY AROUND.

A SILLY REASON

TEN YEARS FROM NOW I WANT (MY PLAYERS) TO LOOK BACK ON COLLEGE AS A WONDERFUL

TO BE SERIOUS

TIME OF EXPANDING THEMSELVES — NOT JUST FOUR YEARS OF PLAYING FOOTBALL."

ABOUT A GAME."

JOE PATERNO